GREAT COMIC CATS

GREAT COMIC
CATS

by Bill Blackbeard and Malcolm Whyte

Foreword by Jim Davis, creator of Garfield

Edited by
Karen Schiller

Book Design by
Nancie Swanberg

Troubador Press San Francisco

To Kitty, Elmer, Felicat, Boots, Kittyrinctum, Sir Thomas, Beethovan, Bowser, Max Factor, Mother Lode, Foggy, Cricket, Butterscotch, Qar, Cugel and Kitty Boz, this book is lovingly dedicated.

Title page art: J.G. Francis, *St. Nicholas*, 1883

Frontispiece: The Cheshire Cat from *Alice in Wonderland* by Lewis Carroll, illustrations by Sir John Tenniel.

Library of Congress Cataloging in Publication Data

Blackbeard, Bill.
   Great Comic Cats.
    Bibliography: p. 154
    Includes index.
    1. Cats—Caricatures and cartoons 2. Wit and humor, Pictorial. I. Whyte, Malcolm, 1933-
II. Title.
NC1763.C35B59   741.5   81-7622
ISBN 0-89844-010   AACR2

FIRST EDITION

      1   2   3   4   5   6   7   8   9   0

FOREWORD

Al Capp once told me it takes two things to be a cartoonist: first, it helps to have been dropped on your head as a small child; second, you must have no desire, talent, or ability to do anything useful in life. There's a certain amount of truth to that...at times I feel a bit silly drawing funny pictures of kitty cats for a living. Perhaps I shouldn't feel that way, after all, there are even sillier people paying me to do it.

Admittedly, cartooning is my first love, and, obviously, cats are another love of mine. But, when I decided to combine the two a few years ago, I was in no way prepared for the reception Garfield® would be given. Cat lovers are the most zealous of all the pet lovers in the world!

People naturally attribute human traits and qualities to cats because cats are so laid back. Not only does one feel that a cat thinks in English, but that it also has the ability to read what is on one's mind. Quite frankly, I treat Garfield as a human in a cat suit. Of all domesticated animals, cats have more of their primal instincts intact. Combining a human personality with a primal animal is intriguing but not all that challenging. Way down deep we are all motivated by the same urges that motivate cats. Cats have the courage to live by them.

While cats are very independent, they seem to demand the devotion of their owners. I have had the opportunity to visit with literally thousands of cat lovers. Sometimes it is hard to tell where the owner leaves off and the cat starts. One best-selling author confided his cat helps him write his novels. Every moment spent at the typewriter involves his cat either sitting on his lap or lying on his shoulder sharing his consciousness and contributing cat energy to the creative flow. Call it anything you like but that cat has helped make his owner a millionaire 'and quite famous to boot.

The late James Dean was from my hometown of Fairmount, Indiana. He privately attributed much of his acting method to the study of cats. As a youth he would mimic the resting, yawning and stretching gestures of his farm cats as a relaxation exercise before his stage appearances. He admired cats for the nervous energy they contained under a thin veneer of passive grace.

A senior executive of a prominent publishing company told of his cat's passion for his wife's piano playing. For fourteen years the cat would curl up atop the piano as Sarah played and never moved 'til she was through. One night, quite elderly and quite ill, the cat crawled onto the keyboard of the piano, buried its face in its paws, and quietly passed away...a testament to its love for her music. I don't know how many times he told that story, but tears still welled up in his eyes as he finished it.

Cats are perfect for comics. They are at once subtle, physical, thoughtful, and slapstick. They have tremendous latitude. Since they aren't obviously of a particular sex, age, or race, they can move into many areas and make comments on many subjects that are restricted for their human counterparts. A cat pummeling a dog is quite natural...a man pummeling a dog is considered bad form. Several of Garfield's personal traits, such as overeating, oversleeping, and not exercising are endearing in cats and disgusting in humans.

Cats are universally loved, hated, feared, and worshipped. Where better to anthropomorphize our furry brothers and sisters than in the comics? While at times they are treated shabbily, other cartoonists give them their due as the thoughtful, graceful, independent creatures they are. Great Comic Cats is a living, loving testament to the affection my compatriots and I have expressed for cats over the years. As Garfield would say, "It's about time."

Jim Davis

ACKNOWLEDGEMENTS

Cover: *Krazy Kat* copyright © King Features Sundicate

Page 5: Foreword by Jim Davis: Copyright © 1981 United Feature Syndicate, Inc.

Page 16: "A Catamaran" reproduced by permission of The Fine Arts Museums of San Francisco

Page 65: From *The Tale of Tom Kitten* by Beatrix Potter, and from *The Pie and the Patty-pan* by Beatrix Potter, reproduced by permission of Frederick Warne and Co., Inc.

Page 66: From *Perrault's Complete Fairy Tales*, with illustrations by W. Heath Robinson, published by Dodd, Mead and Company Inc. Reprinted by permission of the publisher.

Page 115: Reprinted by permission of Coward, McCann and Goeghegan, Inc. from *Millions of Cats* by Wanda Gag. Copyright 1928; renewed © 1956 by Wanda Gag.

Page 116. From *Ring O'Roses* by L. Leslie Brooke, copyright Frederick Warne & Co., Ltd. 1922, 1976, reproduced by permission of Frederick Warne & Co.

Page 117: From *The Pooh Story Book* by A.A. Milne, illustrated by Ernest H. Shepard. Copyright © 1965 by E.P. Dutton & Co., Inc. Reprinted by permission of the publisher, E.P. Dutton.

Page 118: Illustrations by George Herriman, copyright 1933 by Doubleday & Co., Inc. From the book *the lives and times of archy and mehitabel* by don marquis. Reproduced by permission of the publisher.

Page 120: From *The Giant Golden Book of Cat Stories*. Illustrated by Fedor Rojankovsky. Copyright © 1953 Western Publishing Company, Inc. Reprinted by permission.

Page 121: Reprinted by permission of Farrar, Straus and Giroux, Inc. Illustrations from *The Cricket in Times Square* by George Selden, Illustrations by Garth Williams. Illustrations copyright © 1960 by George Selden Thompson and Garth Williams. Illustrations from *Harry Cat's Pet Puppy* by George Selden, Illustrations by Garth Williams. Pictures copyright © 1974 by Garth Williams.

Page 122: Text excerpt and selected illustrations from *No Kiss For Mother*, written and illustrated by Tomi Ungerer. Copyright © 1973 by Tomi Ungerer. By permission of Harper & Row, Publishers, Inc.

Page 123: From the book *Fat Cat* by Jack Kent. Copyright © 1971 by Jack Kent. Reprinted by permission of Four Winds Press, a division of Scholastic Inc.

Page 124-5: Reprinted by permission of Edward Gorey

Page 160: Illustration from "The Cat That Walked in by Himself" copyright 1902 by Rudyard Kipling from *Just So Stories*. Reprinted by permission of the National Trust and Doubleday & Company, Inc.

COMIC STRIPS

Spooky reprinted by permission of the Chicago Tribune-New York News Syndicate, Inc.

Wright Angles, *Gordo*® and *Garfield*® reprinted by permission of United Feature Syndicate, Inc.

Krazy Kat, *Polly and Her Pals*, *The Pussycat Princess* and *Felix the Cat* reprinted by permission of King Features Syndicate

Heathcliff and *Cicero's Cat* reprinted by permission of the McNaught Syndicate

Fritz the Cat reprinted by permission of R. Crumb

Fat Freddy's Cat reprinted by permission of Gilbert Shelton

Special thanks to Larry Evans for his inspiration and guidance in bringing this book to life.

CONTENTS

David Ericson, 1897

There · was · an · old · cat · named · Maria ·
Who · to · sing · to · high · "C" · did · aspire ·
In · the · midst · of · her · wails ·
Came · of · water · two · pails ·
Which · had · previously · been · near · the · fire ·

INTRODUCTION

Cats are sly, stealthy, coy, crafty, cunning, sneaky, supple, and proud. They are also very funny.

We are presently ankle-deep in delectably amusing cat characters—a situation made obvious by the myriad of books, posters, and clothing accessories featuring cats that surround us. The cat is inarguably the second most popular pet in Europe and America and in some areas may very well surpass the dog in general appeal. If people had instead given their hearts (not to mention their homes) to warthogs and badgers and bats, it is doubtful that our libraries would presently house, as they do, shelf after shelf groaning with the weight of cat books. We would doubtless be greeted instead with hordes of lovingly written and illustrated works on warthogs, badgers, or bats. The nursery would gently reverberate with the timeless morality of *Three Little Warthogs*; grandmothers and grandchildren would share the magnificent drama and drawings of *Badger in Boots*; and the lyrical meter of *The Bat in the Hat* would bring tears of fond recognition to generations of now grown-up bat lovers.

But, in fact, it was the common, quarrelsome, sun-basking bantams of the feline family that finally won the human heart and thus prominence in our art as well as at our hearths. *How* this happened is not precisely known, of course. Initially, it was perhaps a matter of the practical and enforced trade Kipling described in "The Cat That Walked by Himself," whereby the cat undertakes to act as *Chief mouser* to a cave woman if given food, water, and shelter in return (the rest of the time the cat walks alone). Cats, obviously recognizing a good thing when they found it, hung around long enough to insure that the statistical household with its two parents, two and one-quarter children, and one-third dog will continue to retain its one-fifth cat.

With the Lords of the Rooftops (as Van Vechten called cats in his book, *The Tiger in The House*) now so deeply snuggled into the lives of human beings, their frequent starring appearances in artistic productions are only to be expected. Representations of these works have been collected again and again in books of all nations. Curiously, however, no considerable chronological collection of cats in caricature and comic narrative has ever been published in English. In fact, very few widely representative anthologies of cat cartoons have been printed *anywhere*, and none at all in recent decades. This volume is an eager attempt to remedy this major referential gap and bring information and pleasure to those interested in cats, comic art, comic narrative, or all three at once.

The human artist, of course, loves to caricature his friends as much as his enemies. It is clearly as the former that cats have been presented in the vast majority of comic drawings from what might be called the contemporary era of Western humorous art (dating roughly from 1775). Although, through the nineteenth and early twentieth centuries, cats sometimes are delineated in distressing predicaments and in far from flattering poses (A. B. Frost's brilliant "The Fatal Mistake," included in this book, is a signal example), such renditions only reflect the generally rough flow of popular humor in those years and indicate no dislike of cats, let alone any real desire to see such indignities inflicted on them. Genuine ailurophobia (fear or hatred of cats) seems scarce in feline caricature and emerges mostly in fearful legends about cats. Thus

Opposite: A.B. Frost, Stuff and Nonsense, *1888.*

C, was a Comical Cat
Who tried to make love to a
She sang him a song [rat.
Both loving, and long,
But he said "You can't fool me
[like that"!

the seeming bias in this work toward delightful comic cats and kittens is not a forced condition, but one encountered almost universally in the available material of the past two centuries.

Cat caricature in cartoons, abundant in the nineteenth century, proliferated even more broadly in the twentieth, thanks largely to the inexpensive products of modern printing and to the American invention of the comic strip. The lucky thousands who were able to buy the works of Frost, Kemble, or Cruikshank a hundred years ago pale against the *millions* who have delighted in the newsprint escapades of such bewhiskered adventurers as Felix, Krazy Kat, Poosy Gato, Spooky, Cicero's Cat, Fritz, Fat Freddy's Cat, and the whole cast of *The Pussycat Princess* from Sargeant Snoop of Scatland Yard to Princess Pauline herself. When people today turn their thoughts to the great comic cats, it is almost invariably and understandably these felicitous figures of the comic section that come leaping and pratfalling to mind. And so, as they should, they cavort large in the text and illustrations of *Great Comic Cats*.

The highly important comic strip area aside, this book also traces the sinuous feline trail through classical art, comic illustrations in children's and adult fiction, political cartoons, and animated cartoons.

In sum, here are well over three hundred classic representations of the great comic cats of the past two hundred years; some in multiple appearances as behooves their importance to art and literature. They are brought to you from the rooftops, back alleys, parlors, and palaces of the imaginary world into your lap to love, laud, and celebrate.

Above: Reginald Birch, famed for decades as one of America's leading children's book illustrators, depicts a lute-strumming cat as part of a comical alphabet drawn for St. Nicholas magazine, March 1884.

Chapter 1   THE FIRST CATS
Ancient to 17th Century Illustration

The Ark on the dark, multitudinous waters
  Was tossing; the rain in a cataract poured;
But Noah, his Lady, their sons and their daughters
  And all the wild live stock were safely aboard.

They weren't much seasick in spite of the weather
  And rather cramped quarters; they'd food to suffice,
And all things were lovely, when, squeaking together,
  There rushed from the galley a rabble of mice!

They multiplied—yes, like a warren of rabbits!
  They plundered the pantry, devoured the grain;
And such were their simply unspeakable habits
  That poor Mrs. Noah was well-nigh insane!

She said so in language untrammeled and forceful!
  And what might have happened, the Lord only knows!
When Noah, the kindly and ever resourceful,
  Went up to the Lion and tickled his nose.

Then thrice sneezed the Lion!—and forth from the feature
  His Majesty sneezed with, there leaped in a trice
A silky-haired, dagger-clawed, brisk little Creature—
  And woe to the ravaging legions of mice!

In twenties, in thirties, in fifties she slew them
  Before Mrs. Noah had time to say "scat"!
"Aha!" laughed the Skipper, who watched her pursue them;
  "I don't know Its name, Dear; let's call it—A Cat!"

So, born of a sneeze in the Rain of All Ages
  That deluged the mountain, the valley, and plain,
The Cat on your hearthstone to this day presages,
  By solemnly sneezing, the coming of rain!

Arthur Guiterman

The droll poem, titled "The First Cat," by Guiterman, above, proposes one origin of cats and their relationship to humankind. We know that the mighty mousers have been around for a very long time. Fossils of the wild cat family have been found going back 35 million years. We have no documentation to *prove* their high comic rating, but we must assume that these antediluvian felines added at least a dash of levity to the otherwise desperate, media-less routine of the cavedweller's day.

No doubt, as far back as the start of human time, stories about cats were told in front of the flame-rosy hearths by oldsters to wide-eyed children. Although these early characterizations must have been largely vocal, cats, comic and otherwise, were also represented in primitive as well as sophisticated art.

Cats were more than just folktale characters in ancient Egypt. They were not only domesticated (about 3000 B.C.) by their hosts on the Nile, but deified as well. Perhaps because of the cats' seemingly occult power to see in the dark, the cat-faced god, Bastet, and other cat effigies graced burial rooms to guide the departed through the afterlife. Since they were a part of Egyptian life, cats also were a part of Egyptian art.

Alfred Freuh, The Log of the Ark, *1915.*

The pampered pets earned their way by controlling the Egyptian rat, mouse, and snake population and were, in turn, rewarded with their own send–off into immortality. Embalmed with spices and wound in colorful cloth, they reposed in elaborately decorated cases. Sometimes even little mouse mummies accompanied the expired puss into the everlasting.

Brought out of Egypt to Europe by Phoenician traders, the valuable rodent-chasers spread across the continent. The Greeks loved cats. Their moon goddess, Artemis, was credited with creating the cat; thus the cat was often associated with the moon. In the sixth century B.C., Aesop gave the cat a literary loft in his fables of animal wisdom.

Cats were introduced into China about 100 B.C.; Japan welcomed them about 600 years later. Chinese legend recounts another charming origin story wherein the cat is a result of a cross between a lioness and a monkey. It is said that the lioness gave the cat dignity, while the monkey imparted curiosity and playfulness.

As history records, these diminutive fur-bearing mischief-makers continued to mingle their fortunes with their fur-less landlord, padding inexorably into his language and art. Artists of no less stature than Ghirlandaio, da Vinci, Dürer and Cellini painted, drew, engraved and sculpted cats; sometimes as a sinister symbol of betrayal and evil; other times as a wondrous nucleus of muscle and sinew, whisker and tail — simply, a cat.

With the invention of movable type and early printing techniques, *Felis catus'* image took a big leap forward. By the 1600s, the story of *Dick Whittington's Cat* again proved the importance of cats to any

Right: Egyptian painting of a cat eating a fish under the chair of its owner, Nakht, scribe and astronomer.

Below: This comic scene dates back to 1100 B.C., a time of poverty and weakness in the Egyptian empire. Painted on papyrus, the art humorously portrays the declining social order.

Londoner who might have doubted it. The cat, the first ever to reach the African shores, brought fame and fortune to her young, penniless master just by being a cat. The story, published in chapbooks (little books sold in the streets by vendors or "chapmen"), was the first ripple on a growing tide of illustrated children's literature that is the wellspring of all the great comic cats.

These exquisite sketches were rendered around 1800 by the Japanese master landscape artist, Hokusai, as part of a page of animal drawings.

Aesop's famous tale of "The Lion and the Mouse" is illustrated in this engraving by Wenceslaus Hollar from The Fables of Aesop, *London, 1665.*

Right: From the notebooks of Leonardo da Vinci, a study of a relaxing cat, drawn in the late 15th century.

Opposite: In Adam and Eve (1504), Albrecht Dürer uses a cat and other animals to symbolize various aspects of human nature.

Right: Dick Whittington's cat chases all the mice out of Africa in this silhouette by Arthur Rackham.

Chapter 2 GRAPHIC CATS
18th and 19th Century Book Illustration

For years, young people learned their ABCs from reading hornbooks (sometimes called "battledores" in England because of their paddle-like shape). These pre-Victorian alphabet slates or single page primers occasionally had illustrations for each letter. And, of course, C is for CAT.

By the early 18th century, book publishing was well under way as a practicable commercial enterprise in western Europe. It was only a matter of time before the process of illustrating printed texts with engraved blocks of wood and metal developed. While such art first appeared in adult works of geography, history, and zoology, its use spread quickly to children's primers, textbooks and storybooks. In England, John Newbery emerged as the first major publisher of children's books, issuing the first book in his Juvenile Library series in 1744.

In the course of turning out simplified art for illustrated books, it was natural for artists to use fabulous and funny animals. In keeping with the traditional attitudes of the times—educational values should prevail over entertainment—animals used to illustrate school texts tended to be rigidly realistic and executed with a minimum of engaging decor.

Opposite: Cats and crones have always been a popular subject for artists. This etching, titled A Catamaran, *was hand colored by Thomas Rowlandson in 1811.*

Right: Hornbooks had an alphabet engraved or printed on a board or paper and protected with a thin, transparent sheet of horn. This example is from 1798.

17

Pre-Victorian graphic art examples. Above: "The Lioness and The Fox", a metal engraving attributed to Elisha Kirkall, London, 1722; Right: Metal etching by James Gillray in 1800 of a favorite subject of the times (see page 23); Below: Wood engraving by Thomas Bewick, late 1700s.

COMFORT to the CORNS.

The technical capabilities of new printing methods and increased distribution touched off an explosion of graphic excellence and comic heights in the pre-Victorian era, the effects of which are still felt today in their influence on contemporary illustration and comic art.

In England, Thomas Bewick (died 1828) brought wood engraving to a pinnacle of precision by carving on the harder grained end of the block, rather than on the softer side. He illustrated ABCs as well as publications such as *Robinson Crusoe, Aesop's Fables,* and *A Pretty Book of Pictures for Little Misters and Misses.* Thomas Rowlandson (1757-1827) drew the very first recurrent comic character, Dr. Syntax, as well as numerous outstanding comic illustrations and prints. James Gillray (1757-1815), a creator of outrageous caricatures, furthered the development of the speech balloon that survives to this day in cartoons. John Leech's (1817-1864) illustrations of world history entertained while they educated, in deft lampoons of society.

One famous and amusing example of this era's comic art featured funny cats and an old lady. *Continuation of the moving adventures of Old Dame Trot and her Comical Cat* first appeared in 1806. In 1823, a slightly different version of the story, this one starring "Dame Wiggins of Lee" was published. John Ruskin, the British critic and sociological writer, read the story as a child and later republished it, with four additional stanzas and illustrations by Kate Greenaway. The art in the 1806 version of the story is particularly interesting, being one of the first examples we see of humanized cats; that is, cats that dressed,

This perfectly balanced little narrative of art and text (pages 19 and 20), resembling pre-comic strip Sunday-supplement material of the close of the century, follows the Mother Hubbardish escapades of Dame Trot, Miss Puss, and Toby to their cozy conclusion. A paperback storybook, it dates from the early 1800s.

THE ADVENTURES OF
DAME TROT AND HER WONDERFUL CAT.

Dame Trot came home one winter's evening quite hungry, and trembling with cold. But her cat had lighted a good fire, and nice roasted a fine fat fowl for the Dame's supper.

Oh how happy the old lady was! the cloth was neatly spread, the juicy fowl smoking on the table ; and this marvellous cat set herself to the duty of carving it up.

DAME TROT AND

When the cloth was removed the Dame exclaimed! what a pity it is not to have something to drink, Miss Puss runs quickly for some wine, and soon returns with a bottle uncorked

But alas! Miss Puss took a glass herself, it soon got in her head ; here she is dancing, capering, throwing somersets, and declaring she won't go to bed.

But all things have an end; and see, the fun over, they have all sunk into a sound and peaceful slumber, excepting that the old lady snores rather loud

Early next morning, Miss Puss awakened the Dame! who found breakfast all ready, and Miss Puss ready to do the honours of the table.

Puss having finished her shaving, dressed herself very gaily with a hat and feather on one side, and a rich crimson dress set off with an elegant tippet

She had just finished when Dame Trot came in, who in admiration made her a very low curtesy, which Puss returned with charming grace.

Breakfast over, Dame Trot went out to visit a neighbour; on her return, she found Miss Puss and her friend Toby engaged in a game of cards.

Another time she came in and found poor Toby with a piteous countenance, seated with his face covered with soap suds, and half of it shaved by the mischievous cat.

And so they lived very happily together for many years, though truth compels me to add, that Miss Puss, though a very great coquette and an acknowledge beauty, remained and died an old maid. She flirted with our friend Toby for many years, but Toby getting tired one day, went off with a mate, which so affected Miss Puss, that she took to her bed, and never got up again.

FINIS.

These two pictures, taken from a much earlier (1806) version of the once-classic Dame Trot jingles, were published in a tiny volume by William Godwin of London. Authorship and artistry were "Attributed to the pen of the Duchess of ***; and illustrated with elegant engravings after Sir Joshua (Reynolds)."

When DAME TROT had dref's'd,
Her Cat very fine,
She called in her Neighbours,
Juft with her to dine.

SOCIABILITY

She went to the Shop,
To get fome nice Pickles,
And when fhe came back,
She was playing at Skittles.

AMUSEMENT

walked, and talked like humans (notice the cat in gown, feathered hat, and fan). Humanized cats became more and more popular in comic art, showing up in children's book illustrations, vignettes, magazine drawings, and finally in their own comic strips.

A Swiss schoolmaster, Rodolphe Töpffer (1788-1846) made great strides in the development of the picture story in strip form. Finally came George Cruikshank (1792-1878), perhaps the grand master of them all. With his true eye and merciless pen, he captured the foibles and fashions of 19th century England so vividly and energetically that his illustrations seem as alive today as ever. Bloated politicians, lean and scheming merchants, ebullient boys, demure young ladies, and sour spinsters with their inseparable companions, cats and kittens, shimmered on the copperplate of Cruikshank and lit the way for all the joyful, playful pages that were to come.

DAME WIGGINS of Lee,
Was a worthy old soul,
As e'er threaded a nee-
dle, or washed in a bowl;
She held mice and rats
In such antipathy,
That seven fine cats
Kept Dame Wiggins of Lee.

So they sat in a tree,
And said "Beautiful! Hark!"
And they listened and looked
In the clouds for the lark.
Then sang, by the fireside,
Symphonious-ly
A song without words
To Dame Wiggins of Lee

Above, left: Obviously derived from the Dame Trot ditties, the 1823 Dame Wiggins of Lee and Her Seven Wonderful Cats, *written by R. S. Sharpe and a Mrs. Pearson and illustrated by R. Stennett, was a considerable improvement as comic art and narrative over the earlier work. The quarter-moon features of Dame Wiggins (reminiscent of the face of Punch) were a standard of the period in rendering the faces of quaint old ladies.*

Above, right: Kate Greenaway, gifted children's book illustrator of the late nineteenth century, hewed closely to Stennett's original lines in redrawing the illustrations for Dame Wiggins *in an 1885 edition of the work published by John Ruskin.*

Right: This humorously eerie anonymous drawing is one of two illustrations in a rare 1807 four page children's book called The Lion's Masquerade. *The text is engaging; one would like to see the rest of this narrative about "the fam'd* learned Pig."

And now at the door was a terrible clatter,
The beasts all about wonder'd what was the matter.
A poor *Cat in pattens* came running so fast,
Her ticket was almost forgot as she past;
But there was, it appear'd, quite enough to alarm her,
For close at her heels came a *great Hog in armour*.
Then follow'd his friend in a very large wig
As a *deep-read Professor*—the fam'd *learned Pig*.

MIXING A RECIPE FOR CORNS

Cats and crone are portrayed with Cruikshank's usual verve in this 1835 etching. Following in the footsteps of his caricaturist father, Isaac, George Cruikshank was considered the leading comic illustrator in 19th century England.

George Cruikshank

Chapter 3   THE QUEEN'S CATS
Victorian Book Illustration

From the London dock cats who barely escaped the slavering jaws of Bill Sikes' dreaded bull terrier in *Oliver Twist* to the multitude of adventurous felines of folktale fame, most Victorian representatives of the genus *felinus* led a vigorous, if not hectic, life. In art as well as reality, the pampered house pets so cherished by maidenly ladies of means and well-to-do households in general were vastly outnumbered by the hordes of alley and farm cats who swarmed through the wet brick streets of cities or padded over the warm straw floors of country barns without belonging to anyone in particular, and who searched as much for an occasional caress as an accidentally dropped tidbit. It was not until the twentieth century and a general rise in the standard of living for most English families that many of England's roaming cats were taken into familial bosoms, and the occasional stray cat became a distinct rarity.

Things were not better for American cats in those years either, if one is to judge from the cruel humor with which they are treated in the comic papers and literature as exemplified by A.B. Frost's comic horror, *The Fatal Mistake* (pages 42-43). Mark Twain's Tom Sawyer was benign in spooning croup medicine down the throat of Aunt Polly's cat (with the classic result we all know) when compared to the sometimes unspeakable treatment accorded cats by the nominally comic characters of such rough-and-ready writers of Twain's time as Billy Nye, Ambrose Bierce, and Petroleum V. Nasby. Yet the furry darlings prevailed in the long run, becoming in a few decades as intimate, respected, and beloved a part of the American domestic scene as they had become in England.

In Victorian caricature, cats ran the gamut from the cadaverous, feral, mischievous beasts of George Cruikshank (opposite) to the cuddly, tumbling, cream-filled kittens of children's books (page 28) whose purpose was to draw youngsters into reading as well as to demonstrate the proficiencies of ever-improving printing techniques. Besides their portrayal as absurd or destructive nuisances on the one hand or idealized family pets on the other, cats were also shown as *humanized* creatures in folklore, fairy tales, social satire, and instructive works for children. Anthropomorphic cat characters were, however, not introduced in major adult works (as they were to be in the twentieth century), and there were no Victorian cat characters developed on the level of Dickens's Pickwick, Mrs. Gamp, Pecksniff, Micawber or Thackerey's Colonel Newcome, or even Edward Lloyd's penny-dreadful villain, Sweeney Todd. Humanized cats, however, such as the perenially popular and mythic figures Puss-in-Boots, the Robber Kitten, Dick Whittington's Cat and other others made repeated appearances in children's books and magazines.

Opposite: This vigorously imagined saturnalia of rampaging cats is also by George Cruikshank. The etching is an illustration titled "The Cat did it!" from The Greatest Plague of Life: or the Adventures of a Lady in search of a good servant, *published in 1847.*

Right: Famous for his biting attacks on the Boss Tweed gang as embodied by the ferocious Tammany Tiger, Thomas Nast was also noted for his creations of the Republican elephant, the Democratic donkey, and the fat and jolly visage of Santa Claus as we know him today. Below: The cozy scene from Christmas Drawings for The Human Race (1889) shows Nast's benign draftsmanship in marked contrast to his Tammany cartoons.

An utterly concentrated cat plucks at a yarn bag under the feet of Mrs. Gamp, Chuffy, Augustus Moddle, Charity Pecksniff and other comic personalities from Charles Dickens's marvelous 1844 comic novel, Martin Chuzzlewit. The drawing was done to Dickens's close instruction by Hablot Knight Browne (Phiz), Cruikshank's nearest rival.

Comic cats portrayed for adults in fiction and accompanying art tended to be either stylized humanistics figures developed to satirize specific human foibles—as in J.J. Grandville's feline people in the French *Les Animaux* of 1842 (pages 30 and 31)—or minimally described lap pets or alley rovers introduced to counterpoint the human characters.

The Cheshire Cat in *Alice in Wonderland* was one of the first vocal and fully developed comic cat characters in English literature to be as widely appreciated by adults as by children. No longer a humanized cat in terms of costume, but deeply human in spirit, the Cheshire Cat had a particularly good-humored point of view. The cat always appeared friendly toward Alice, although—properly for a cat—distant (if not invisible). Its materialization at the Queen of Hearts' croquet ground was a great comfort to Alice—a friendly face in a very disquieting environment. Despite the cat's seemingly maniacal grin, adults recognized a creature of wry, but sane, perspective in a mad, mad world. The Cheshire Cat smiled patiently at the human's foibles, and the readers laughed in recognition of themselves.

Major artists carried into the Victorian era the graphic excitement begun in the 18th century. They graced the munificently illustrated novels and children's books with a generous selection of lovingly rendered comic cats.

In America, Thomas Nast brought the house down on scandalous Boss Tweed with his searing cartoons featuring the Tammany Tiger. English artists George Cruikshank, Edward Lear, and J.G. Francis each demonstrated unique insight into the cat as story embellishment, poetic foil and outright comic device. Sir John Tenniel breathed life into the Cheshire Cat. On the continent, French artist Gustave

These finely detailed pages are part of a small book of The Three Little Kittens, *published by Thomas Nelson & Sons in 1857. The artist was known only as "Comus," but the style is characteristic of Victorian children's book illustrations.*

Doré lent his august mastery to children's storybooks. Germany's Wilhelm Busch, one of the very first purely comic artists, delighted his audience with slapstick serial picture stories that were the inspiration for many future comic strips.

As literacy spread, the demand for books increased, and it became obvious that there was an even greater demand for illustrated volumes. The increased sales far outweighed the extra expense of printing the pictures. This same principle generally operated when color was added to the illustrations.

While most early illustrated children's books contained black and white pictures, they sometimes were available in hand-colored editions. The coloring was usually performed by teenagers gathered around a table, each youngster applying one specific water color to the same part of each printed sheet, be it bow, bonnet, cap, gown, cat, or hat.

By the 1860's, printing in color dominated English picture book publishing, with printer Edmund Evans's outstanding achievements leading the way. Through the newly perfected medium of chromolithography (printing color from limestone plates), inexpensive color-illustrated books such as *Aunt Louisa* and *Aunt Judy* flourished.

By sharing and exchanging color plates, publishers, such as George Routledge and Sons in London and McLoughlin Brothers in New York, could save costs and enthrall both of their young readerships with the same bountifully colored books (page 35). These antique illustrations projected an unabashed vibrance of color, a rich balance of tone, and a raw vitality of texture that is impossible to duplicate today.

Jean-Ignace-Isadore Gerard, *who signed his often hallucinatory and always bizarre drawings of animals and men as J.J. Grandville, was perhaps the most distinctively novel 19th century French artist in black-and-white media. Widely noted today for his continually reprinted cuts in* The New York Review of Books, *Grandville was essentially an "artist's artist" in his own time, exciting his peers with the imaginative span of his work, but sparking little response from a generally baffled or appalled public. The cat character drawings below and on the next page were originally done for* Scenes From the Public and Private Lives of the Animals, *published in Paris in 1842. The picture to the right is from* Fables de La Fontaine *(1738).*

Ses manières étaient celles d'un Chat qui a vu la Cour et le beau monde.
(His manners were those of a Cat who had seen the Court and the beautiful world.)

Lève-toi, et suis-moi, disait la première voix....
(Celle de mon mauvais génie, sans doute.)

(Rise and follow me, said the first voice....
(That of my bad side, no doubt.)

Mon silence l'enhardit, et il s'ecria: Chère Minette!
(My silence emboldened him, and he cried: Dear Minette!)

Designed & Etched by - George Cruikshank - 1864

A pair of Perrault's Puss-In-Boots demonstrate the divergent viewpoints of their respective artists. Above: Cruikshank's puss is caricatured along with the rest of the cast. Opposite: The eloquent 19th century French illustrator, Gustave Doré, chose a grandly dramatic portrayal of this classic hero.

SIR ROUSER'S ARRIVAL

Above: This delicately detailed plate from Old Nursery Stories *(1892) is notable for its charming evocation of period decor. Opposite: Another Puss-in-Boots appeared in* Fairy Legends *from the favorite* Aunt Louisa's *children's book series. Both illustrations exhibit the unique texture and color found in Victorian chromolithography.*

The Prophet of Spring

Old Groundhog said: "Six weeks 'till Spring;"
The Robin came, but froze his wing
And Bluebird vainly tried to sing,
For still the air was chill, oh chill.

Then who will say when skies will clear,
When there's an end of winter drear,
And when mild spring is surely here?
Why, little Pussy Willow will.

36

Opposite: From The Bandit Mouse and Other Tales *by W.A. Frisbie, illustrated by Fred R. Bartholomew (Bart), this visual pun sets a proper tone of sedate Victorian humor.*

The immortal English master of the limerick, Edward Lear, also commanded a madly comic flair as demonstrated in the lunatic prowler depicted below and right.

Fox Couchant

C was a lovely Pussy Cat; its eyes were large & pale; And on its back it had some stripes, and several on his tail.

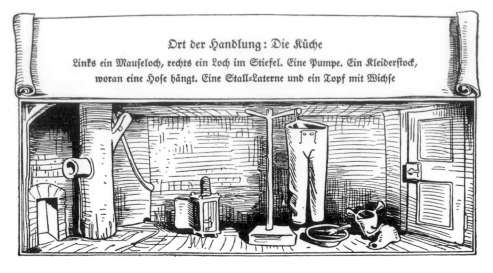

Ort der Handlung: Die Küche

Links ein Mauseloch, rechts ein Loch im Stiefel. Eine Pumpe. Ein Kleiderstock, woran eine Hose hängt. Eine Stall=Laterne und ein Topf mit Wichse

Wilhelm Busch created many picture storybooks, the most popular of which featured the devilish pranksters, Max and Moritz, who in turn were the models for The Katzenjammer Kids— Hans and Fritz. The frantic pace of this cat and mouse story is vintage Busch: In the end the cat is spanked, the stains wash out, and the mice celebrate an escape from the holey boot.

Die Maus spaziert in die Laterne,
Der böse Kater siehts von ferne.

Schnapp! springt er zu: das Glas zerbricht;
Die Maus, die kriegt er aber nicht.

Den Kleiderstock erklimmt die Maus,
Der Kater nach in einem Saus.

Hier sausen sie durchs Hosenbein,
Die Maus heraus, die Katz hinein.

Klatsch! fällt der Kater mit dem Kopf
In einen schwarzen Wichsetopf.

Der Kater ist ein halber Mohr,
Die Maus springt in das Stiefelrohr.

38

Die Köchin und der Hausknecht sehn
Mit Staunen an, was hier geschehn.

Und beide sieht man mit Bemühn
Am Katzenschwanz und Stiefel ziehn.

Pardauz! Da haben wir es ja!
Sie liegen alle beide da.

Der Kater, ders verdient gehabt,
Wird eingeklemmt und abgeklappt.

Und wenn sich einer schwarz gemacht,
Mit Wasser wirds heraus gebracht.

Die Mäuse aber springen   Der brave Stiefel hat ein Loch!
Im Kreis herum und singen: Der Stiefel lebe! Vivat hoch!

SCENE I.   SCENE II.

Above: One of the St. Nicholas cartoonists most inclined to develop comic cat material was the prolific J. G. Francis. The two cuts on this page are from Francis's work in 1882. Note, unlike the serial form of Busch, Francis' art is beginning to approach a comic strip look. The verse below is also by Francis.

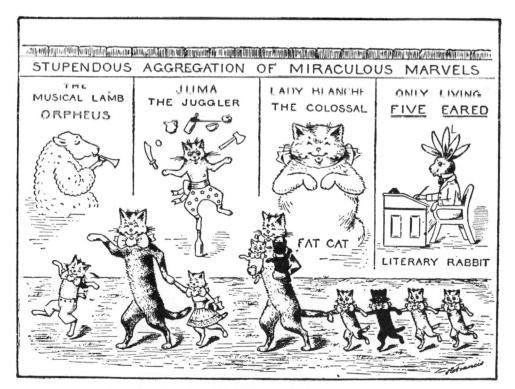

Cried a Cat to his Wife, "See, my dear,
The superlative Circus is here.
    With the children we'll go,—
    'Tis our duty, you know,
Their young minds to enlighten and cheer."

The · Fatal · Mistake

A · Tale · of · a · Cat ·

The superbly structured graphic narrative that appears on these two pages is widely considered to be the foremost comic work of its creator, A.B. Frost. The sequence first appeared in Frost's book Stuff and Nonsense, 1888.

1

2

3

4

5

6

7

8

9

10

THE TALE OF A TUB.

I.

Two dear friends sat down to tea;
And both were sleek and fair to see.

II.

All went well until one spied
Great danger near. "Oh, look!" she cried.

III.

A furious, uninvited beast
Was rushing madly to the feast.

IV.

Quick as a flash they had him under,
Ere he "Jack Robinson" could thunder.

V.

Then safely from a tall careppa
They saw their dwelling play Mazeppa.

VI.

Departed foe! Delighted friends!
And so this thrilling story ends.

Chapter 4 PERIODICAL CATS

Victorian Magazine Illustration

Victorian humor magazines proliferated on both sides of the Atlantic. England boasted the grandest of them all—*Punch*. Among others were the less erudite *Ally Sloper's Weekly* and the longest running competitor to *Punch* called—what else?—*Judy*. Readers in America chuckled at the often coarse jokes in *Life*, *Judge*, *Truth*, and *Puck*. The buoyant, if not raffish, wit of these magazines was primarily adult, satirizing social, religious and political mores.

Periodicals for Victorian children were very few; in fact, in the early part of the era they didn't exist at all. It wasn't until the late 1800s that *The River Magazine*, *Our Young Folks*, and *Harper's Round Table* appeared. In November 1873, the first issue of *St. Nicholas* magazine for children was published by the Century Company in New York. Under the imaginative editorship of Mary Mapes Dodge, *St. Nicholas* engaged boys and girls for two generations with wholesome, joyous, adventurous fare. Amid the stories, pictures, factual essays, poems, riddles, jokes, and games sparkled the creations of the best artists and writers of the time—and cats were a favorite theme. Rudyard Kipling penned his first *Just So Stories* for the magazine. Longfellow, Whittier, Tennyson, Mark Twain, Bret Harte, and Theodore Roosevelt were just a few of the other contributors to *St. Nicholas*.

Opposite: "Boz" penned this slapstick farce worthy of Max Sennett. (Mazeppa, it might be noted, was an Indian maiden who was tied to a runaway horse in the recurrent Victorian stage melodrama.) The page ran in St. Nicholas, *October 1890.*

Right: Culmer Barnes, represented by an October 1884 St. Nicholas *vignette, introduces individuality and believable human postures in his otherwise wholly realistic cats.*

The Audacious Kitten.

BY OLIVER HERFORD.

"HURRAY!" cried the kitten, "hurray!"
  As he merrily set the sails;
"I sail o'er the ocean to-day
  To look at the Prince of Wales!"

"O kitten! O kitten!" I cried,
  "Why tempt the angry gales?"
"I 'm going," the kitten replied,
  "To look at the Prince of Wales!"

"O kitten! pause at the brink,
  And think of the sad sea tales."
"Ah, yes," said the kitten, "but think,
  Oh, think of the Prince of Wales!"

"But, kitten!" I cried, dismayed,
  "If you live through the angry gales
You *know* you will be afraid
  To look at the Prince of Wales!"

"I know what it is to get wet,
  I 've tumbled full oft in pails
And nearly been drowned — and yet
  I *must* look at the Prince of Wales!"

"O kitten!" I cried, "the Deep
  Is deeper than many pails!"
Said the kitten, "I shall not sleep
  Till I 've looked at the Prince of
    Wales!"

Said the kitten, "No
    such thing!
  Why should he make
    me wince?
If '*a Cat may look at a
    King*,'
A kitten may look at a
  Prince!"

Oliver Herford, who wrote and illustrated the once-famed Rubiayat of a Persian Kitten, *was a leading artist in the comic development of cats in both lyrics and art. In the two fine examples of his* St. Nicholas *work here and on the next page, Herford first illustrates a set of his own verses in the issue of August 1890 and then devotes his skill to illustrating some lines by Carolyn Wells. Wells, famed at this time for her humorous sketches and verse, was later acclaimed for her numerous mystery novels.*

A Serious Question.
carolyn Wells

A KITTEN went a-walking
  One morning in July,
And idly fell a-talking
  With a great big butterfly.

The kitten's tone was airy,
  The butterfly would scoff;
When there came along a fairy
  Who whisked his wings right off.

And then,—for it is written
  Fairies can do such
    things,—
Upon the startled kitten
  She stuck the yellow
    wings.

The kitten felt a quiver,
  She rose into the air,
Then flew down to the river
  To view her image there.

With fear her heart was smitten,
  And she began to cry:
"Am I a butter-kitten?
  Or just a kitten-fly?"

*Above, opposite: These pictures illustrated an August 1876 St. Nicholas
story by "A Young Contributor." The pictures are fine examples of realistic
animals in fantasy situations—a favorite Victorian theme. The story, titled
"Brave Tim, the Centennial Cat," is condensed on the next page.*

Brave Tim, the Centennial Cat

Tab, Tim, and Puss were a family of cats living in Pleasant-town. Tab, the mother, died and left Tim and Puss to seek their own living. They first wandered down to a pretty little brook, where they sat and watched the shining perch glide swiftly by. They wished that they could catch some, for they were very hungry. Finding their wishes were vain, they fell asleep.

Not far from the brook was a circus. The music and the general noise woke the kittens. Puss began to mew sadly, but Tim, who was brave and daring, started for the circus grounds.

They found a hiding-place near a great balloon. After a fine meal, Puss fell asleep, while Tim cut all the capers he could think of.

As the balloon took off, Tim, not knowing his danger, was holding tightly to the rope which hung from the basket. Tim was brave and would not let go.

Tim decided to see the world. The men in the balloon's basket took him in, and he could see the great "Centennial" fair from the air.

His new friend took him home to be a plaything for the children, but he was determined to see the fair. The next morning he borrowed a pair of baby boots, a large paper collar, and some red, white, and blue ribbons and proudly strutted off to the Centennial grounds, where he amazed and delighted the throng of curiosity seekers.

"YOU MAKE SO MUCH NOISE I CAN'T SLEEP!"

As a child, Mary Mapes Dodge never went to school, but was instructed at home, with her two sisters, by tutors and governesses in English, French, Latin, music, and drawing. Her interest in drawing is clearly revealed by the excellent pageant of art adorning *St. Nicholas*. She attracted the talents of Oliver Herford, Reginald Birch, Palmer Cox, Harrison Cady, Howard and Catherine Pyle, and Frederick Richardson (whose wondrous illustrations accompanied a serialization of L. Frank Baum's *Queen Zixi of Ix*). Some of the earliest work of Norman Rockwell enriched the pages of this beloved magazine.

The pictures on this page illustrated an October 1891 St. Nicholas *article about artist J.H. Dolph, "An Artist Who Loves Cats and Dogs and Paints Them."*

A Composite Cat.

By Maria J. Hammond.

We took our pussy's photograph,
  Then one of a neighbor's cat,
And then a third, and then a fourth,—
  A dozen pussies sat.
And then we took the photograph
  Of every photograph;
Oh, that is often done, you know;
  Indeed you need n't laugh!

We showed Mamma the last effect.
  " Here is the type," we said,
" Of all the dozen pussy cats —
  See what a splendid head!"
" Splendid? A terror!" cried Mamma,—
  Quite frank, to say the least.
" Each puss would be a truer type
  Than this composite beast!"

St. Nicholas, *November 1888.*

Readers of today are most familiar with Mrs. Dodge as the author of *Hans Brinker or The Silver Skates*, which was published several years before she edited *St. Nicholas*. She had great insight into young people, because through all her years of responsibilities, cares, and triumphs, she retained to the end the heart of a child. In her own words, Mary Mapes Dodge believed children...

> want to enter the one place where they may come and go as they please, where they are not obliged to mind, or say "yes, ma'am" and "yes, sir"—where, in short, they can live a brand-new, free life of their own for a little while...

Youngsters curled up with the latest *St. Nicholas* and their favorite cat not only found that moment of freedom, but also a lifetime of inspiration to goodness, truth and beauty to influence their young minds and thus the future.

Beside the comic and antic humanized cats romping through children's books and magazines, there were many picture stories lionizing realistic cats and kittens. Engraving and printing technicians were so deft in the graphic media that the illustrated animals seemed to almost roll, skitter and tumble right off the page. With the death of Queen Victoria in 1901, the era faded, and the twentieth century blossomed in a glittering beam of optimism and invention.

KITTEN, WHO HAS BEEN TOLD NEVER TO BE AFRAID OF A RAT: "OW-W! NO FAIR! I WANT TO STOP!"

*Opposite and above, left: Two vignettes drawn by the anonymous "Chip."
The "short lesson" appeared in* Life, *January 3, 1889, and the boxing scene is
from* St. Nicholas, *May 1882. Above, right: W.D. Stevens illustrated a story
by Felix Leigh titled "A Delectable Land from a Boy's Point of View,"* St.
Nicholas, *1896. Below: Sequential art by A.J. Brenton,* St. Nicholas,
March 1889.

BY A BRENON: NINE LITTLE PICTURES OF A BLACK-AND-WHITE CAT AND A PINK WORSTED BALL.

"Another of those horrid flies I suppose".

"Why, nothing of the sort! But a lovely pink worsted ball".

"what a charming play-thing".

"Very kind of someone I am sure to leave this dangling here for me".

"There now, pray don't think you can get away from me".

"See? I told you that you couldn't."

"Come, don't do this now: don't be disagreeable!"

"Thunder! and Mars! This is frightful—Mariar!?"

"The utter stupidity of some folks would amaze a camel; — leaving these hateful worsted balls dangling about to annoy one."

A QUEER PLANT —   OF THE CAT-TAIL VARIETY.

"LET 'S SEE IF IT 'S ANYTHING GOOD TO EAT"   ——!!!

*Two vignettes from St. Nicholas: Above: March,
1893. Below: "Boz" again, July 1883.*

THE CAT AND THE MOUSE.

BY PALMER COX.

The irrepressible Palmer Cox, best known for his 19th and early 20th century drawings and narratives of comic brownies, tackles a cat-and-mouse gag of great antiquity but handles it with some refreshing touches (nicest of which, perhaps, is the mouse braced inside the shaken jar in fig. III). The drawing first appeared in St. Nicholas, November 1882.

BACK FROM THE CONCERT.

Mrs. Thomas de Catt—Were any gifts show-
ered on you, after you struck the high C?

Mr. Thomas de Catt—Nothing of value, my
dear; only a bootjack, two bottles, an old
shoe-brush, and three tomato-cans.

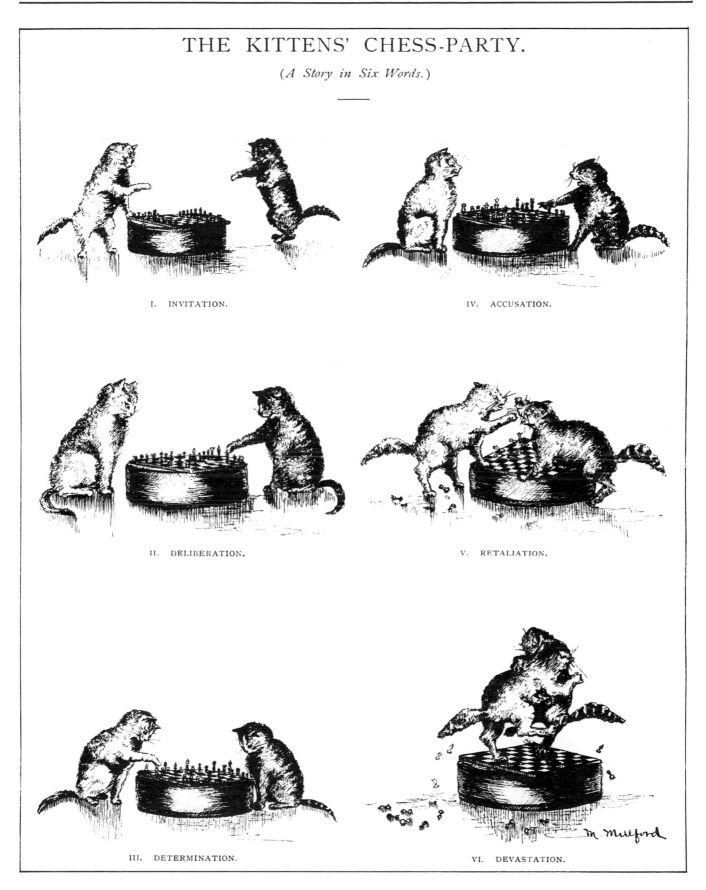

THE KITTENS' CHESS-PARTY.

(A Story in Six Words.)

I. INVITATION.

IV. ACCUSATION.

II. DELIBERATION.

V. RETALIATION.

III. DETERMINATION.

VI. DEVASTATION.

Opposite: E.W. Kemble cartooned for many of the top American humor magazines during the Victorian era, but he's also honored for illustrating the first edition (1884) of The Adventures of Huckleberry Finn. *This picture appeared in St. Nicholas, December 1892.*

Above: More realistic cats in fantasy situations: St. Nicholas, August 1903.

THE LITTLE KITTENS' SURPRISE

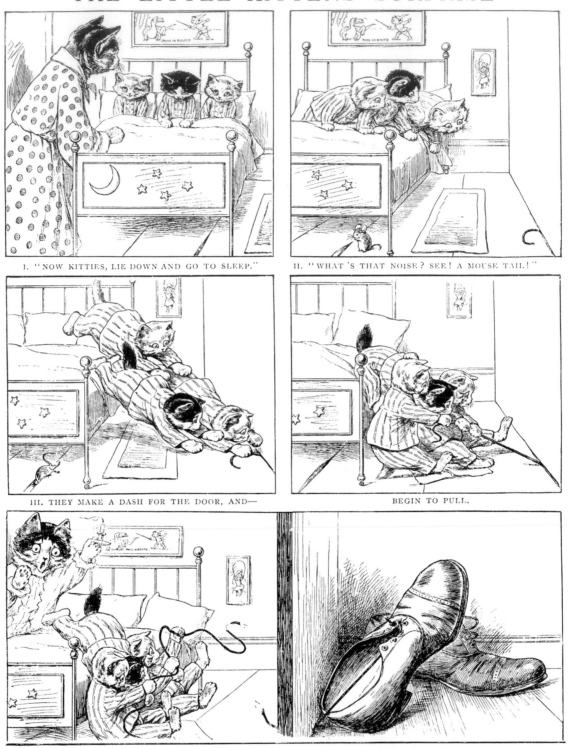

I. "NOW KITTIES, LIE DOWN AND GO TO SLEEP."

II. "WHAT 'S THAT NOISE? SEE! A MOUSE TAIL!"

III. THEY MAKE A DASH FOR THE DOOR, AND—

BEGIN TO PULL.

NOW, "ALL TOGETHER!"—

BUT THIS IS WHAT IT WAS.

The comic skills of Culmer Barnes, one of the most consistent contributors to St. Nicholas, is exhibited on this and the following pages. Note how the picture sequencing reflects the influence of the movies, until it becomes a movie itself.

THE ADVENTURES OF THREE LITTLE KITTENS

"HURRAH! WE ARE GOING TO SEE THE WORLD!"

"OH DEAR, THIS IS DREADFUL!"

"YES, IT IS SWEET MILK; IT 'S YOUR TURN NEXT."

BUT THEY MADE SUCH A NOISE THAT—

JACK CAME OUT AND SO FRIGHTENED THEM THAT—

THEY RAN HOME AS FAST AS THEY COULD GO.

MR. THOMAS CATT'S MOTOR OUTING

HE EXCEEDED THE SPEED LIMIT

AND THOUGHT IT GREAT FUN

UNTIL THE MACHINE STOPPED.

LITTLE TIME WAS LOST HOWEVER.

THE NEXT DAY TOM BOUGHT ANOTHER MACHINE BUT HIS FRIENDS WOULD NOT RIDE WITH HIM AGAIN—THEY SAID HE WAS TOO RECKLESS.

FIRST EXHIBITION OF MOVING PICTURES IN KITTENTOWN

I.

II.

III.

IV.

V.

VI.

Chapter 5 LITERARY LIONS
Book Illustration from 1900 to 1914

The French called it *La belle époque* and what an epoch it was. It was a fresh century, and everywhere the old was giving way to the new.

In 1901, in an orderly transition of government, England crowned Edward VII as her new monarch, and in the same year, Teddy Roosevelt became 26th president of the United States. His flamboyance, energy, and enthusiasm personified the mood of the times. Thanks to Marconi's incredible invention, the first transatlantic radio telegraph transmission was sent and the world shrank a little.

Even the sky wasn't the limit anymore. From Kitty Hawk, North Carolina, in 1903, Orville Wright manned the first successful power-driven aircraft flight. Concurrently, feverish ingenuity had changed the "horseless carriage" into the automobile. A whole family could venture together onto the open road—in style.

At the 1904 St. Louis World's Fair, America celebrated the dawn of the century with her neighbors, near and far. Miracles and curios, scientific and fictional, reverberated under spectacular architecture to the resolute marches of John Philip Sousa and the jubilant ragtime of Scott Joplin.

The period of 1900 to 1909 also fostered unprecedented experimentation in art and children's illustrated books. Vivid and dynamic, the drawings of W.W. Denslow, especially those for L. Frank Baum's Oz books, show a positive influence of the Expressionist movement.

Among the many fantastic and lovable characters inhabiting the Land of Oz, the Cowardly Lion ranks as the most charming, irresistible, and unforgettable. Along with the Cheshire Cat, Dorothy's tawny companion is one of the most favorite felines in literature. In contrast to Cheshire's enigmatic authority, Cowardly's temperament is obvious and vulnerable. He is a good-humored satire on the King of Beasts (and perhaps other monarchs, as well); a more cuddly king couldn't be asked for as he captures the heart of generation after generation of devoted readers.

Right and opposite: These drawings are by W.W. Denslow from L. Frank Baum's The Wonderful Wizard of Oz *(1889).*

Above: A fiercely natural cat tackles its feathered prey with gusto in the first of these two exquisite drawings by the renowned British artist Arthur Rackham, for an English edition of Aesop's Fables (1909). Right: In the second a dexterously humanized cat calls on some birds in the guise of a doctor. Below: Noah sadly deposits a pair of love birds to the interest of his ubiquitous cats, Log of the Ark by Al Frueh, 1915.

Kittens and cats by Beatrix Potter. Above: Tom Kitten *(1907); Below:* The Pie *and* The Patty-pan *(1905). Potter drew her inspiration from studying her pets and the stuffed specimens at the Natural History Museum in London. Even dressed up, the cats retain their natural physiognomy.*

Greatly admired in his time and gaining fresh recognition today among collectors of illustrated books, W. Heath Robinson was one of the most adept and graphically witty British book illustrators at the turn of the century. Especially noted for his children's book work, Robinson is represented here with two drawings from "Puss-in-Boots," in his Perrault's Complete Fairy Tales, 1909.

"Puss became a personage of great importance"

Der liederliche Zimmerherr.

Two comic cat creations from Germany. Above: A slovenly carouser by Kathe Olshausen-Schonberger, famed for her animal fantasies of the pre-World War I period (from Im Spiegel der Tierwelt, *1914). Below: One of the infrequent incorporations of tigers into the stunning line drawings of the still-famed turn-of-the-century German cartoonist, Heinrich Kley.*

The Son-in-law
Der Schwiegersohn

This illustration and the ones on the next page are by Hungarian-born artist Willy Pogany, illustrating Edward Lear's "The Owl and The Pussycat."

Photoengraving and four-color process printing arose at the turn of the century as an alternative to limestone lithography. Fast and accurate, these new techniques were especially effective for reproducing full color illustrations, such as watercolors and oil paintings. Arthur Rackham, Edmund Dulac, W. Heath Robinson, N.C. Wyeth, and Kay Nielsen were some of the artists who took advantage of the new developments. The delicate watercolor paintings of Beatrix Potter were both a challenge to and a triumph of the four-color process technology. Printers could now faithfully reproduce the subtle hues and gentle nature of Peter Rabbit, Jemima Puddle-Duck, Miss Moppet, and Tom Kitten, bringing to them a blushing essence of life.

While some of the color work served in luxury book printing, much appeared in cheap magazines, annuals, and children's books. Black and white artistry still prevailed, and the artists who worked in color also provided a generous share of line work to the expanding published materials. Even Rube Goldberg, a central figure in the Golden Age of comic strips, lent his restless verve to the illustrated book *A Night Out* (page 71), the hilarious saga of a rowdy alley cat.

Children, comics, and cats were becoming inseparable.

THE Owl and the Pussy-Cat went
    to sea
    In a beautiful pea-green boat,
  They took some honey, and plenty
    of money,
Wrapped up in a five-pound note.

They dinèd on mince and slices of quince,
    Which they ate with a runcible spoon ;
And hand in hand, on the edge of the sand,
    They danced by the light of the moon,
        The moon,
They danced by the light of the moon.

Edward Lear

" 'YOUR GOOD HEALTH,' SAID THE DOG"

John R. Neill's bandit cat is toasted by a brigand dog in this scene from The Robber Kitten of 1904. Neill (who often signed himself "Jno" rather than "John") was the illustrator of the majority of L. Frank Baum's Oz books, taking over Denslow's split with Baum following publication of The Wizard of Oz and creating the classic images of two of Baum's most notable comic cats —the Glass Cat in The Patchwork Girl of Oz and Eureka in Dorothy and the Wizard in Oz.

Opposite: Rube Goldberg, the American cartoonist, famed through much of this century for his contrived inventions and the comic strip character, Boob McNutt, drew this piquant sketch for the cover of Edward Peple's short account of a novice cat out on the town for the first time, in his best-selling A Night Out, 1911.

Above: Merle Johnson, an American illustrator, is at the top of his form in this sketch of a determined kitten pursuing a lackey for a lovely, Oz-patterned children's book of 1908, authored by Frederic Chapin and titled Toodles of Treasure Town and Her Snow Man.

"The Beast has had the time of his life."

Chapter 6 SLAPSTICK CATS

Comic Strip Cats from 1900 to 1939

The San Francisco Academy of Comic Art defines the comic strip as: *a recurrently published pictorial narrative or serial with continuing characters, distinguished by expository dialogue set forth immediately adjacent to the source.* It is the unique combination of all these factors that differentiate the modern comic strip from all previous graphic story-telling devices.

By the turn of the century, the golden era of comic strips was dawning. Newspapers were becoming enormously widespread, and competitive publishers W.R. Hearst and Joseph Pulitzer fought fair and foul for domination in the medium. Persevering, gifted, mostly self-taught artists migrated from the country and small towns to New York, Philadelphia and San Francisco to market their talents. Rube Goldberg, James Swinnerton, R.F. Outcault, TAD (Thomas A. Dorgan), George Herriman, and Bud Fisher were just a few artists of the burgeoning great comic strips. Some of these strips would bear great comic cats. October 18, 1896 saw the launching of the first definitive comic strip. On that day, Robert F. Outcault's flap-eared, gap-toothed, grimy, grinning ragamuffin appeared in a blaze of yellow ink, catching the eye and breath of an amazed public. The sensation that the Yellow Kid stirred proved that comics could sell newspapers, and cartoonists responded to their mass audience with a torrent of gleeful creativity.

The first comic strip cat was Mr. Jack, appearing in Hearst's *New York Journal* in 1899. Drawn by James Swinnerton, this orange and black-striped, urban, woman-chasing, bachelor tiger enjoyed a widely enthusiastic readership for over forty years.

Opposite: Felix movie ad first appeared in the Chicago Daily Tribine July 18, 1933.

Right: Mr. Jack drawn by James Swinnerton.

73

Above: In the words of H.G. Wells, Englishman Louis Wain "invented a cat style, a cat society, a whole cat world" for 50 years, even during his last fifteen years in asylums. This 1907 example is from his three-year stint with the Hearst papers.

Not until 1910, however, when George Herriman began the slow evolvement of a minor feline character in a human fantasy strip called *The Family Upstairs* into the heroine of the immortal *Krazy Kat*, did a domestic cat appear regularly on the newspaper strip pages. Four years later, Paw Perkins's Kitty stalked with upright dignity into the hearts of the readers of Cliff Sterrett's *Polly and Her Pals*, to be followed a decade later by the capering hero of *Felix the Cat* (bylined by Pat Sullivan from the start in 1923, but actually drawn by Jack Bogle and Otto Messmer at different times), whose title character stepped from the silent movie screen onto the comic page, twirling his frequently detached tail like Charlie Chaplin's bamboo cane. Still another decade on, in the early 1930s, three of the most memorable comic cats of the American funny pages made their bows almost simultaneously: Cicero's Cat, in a strip of the same name created by Al Smith while working for Mutt and Jeff's creator, Bud Fisher; the Pussycat Princess, conceived by Grace Drayton in the strip of that name and carried on by Ruth Carroll; and Spooky, originally the firehouse cat in Bill Holman's *Smokey Stover*, who quickly acquired a separate strip named for her on the Sunday page. By 1940, with all of these strips still appearing regularly in hundreds of newspapers across the country, it was clear that cats had clowned their way into the comics for good.

Skippy

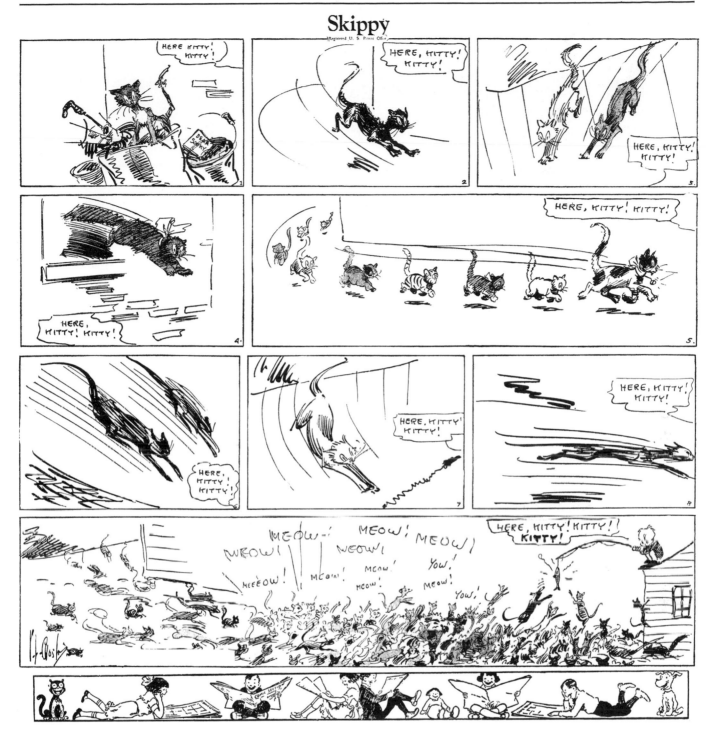

Above: Whether fishing for fish or for cats, boyhood life was deftly portrayed for twenty years in Percy Crosby's strip Skippy; this example dates from 1930.

Opposite, below: This radio page strip, The Radio Catts, *is of interest because it's Chester Gould's first strip. Gould, who also created* Dick Tracy, *drew it in 1924.*

KRAZY KAT

Acclaimed as one of the world's greatest comic cats, Krazy Kat first appeared as a minor figure in George Herriman's *The Dingbat Family* (later *The Family Upstairs*). Herriman created a tailpiece for the strip, in which he involved the family animals (a cat and a bulldog). A mouse also often sneaked in to sock the cat with a stone.

Until 1913, the cat, mouse, and dog team remained part of the larger strip. But finally, on Tuesday, October 28, 1913, the first episode of *Krazy Kat* appeared in the *New York Journal* (the title of the strip being the disparaging term that the often-frustrated mouse used to describe the love-stricken cat).

Krazy Kat was a hit, and Herriman started doing a Sunday page in which he could allow his graphic and poetic fancy to flower. He dazzled his readers with backgrounds that came apart in every panel, fluidly shifting scenes, and the stark angular shapes of the American deserts. The simple vaudeville of the daily strip blossomed into a grand opera of color and shape on Sunday.

Pleased with the response of his readers, Herriman built up the daily strip until it equaled his Sunday extravaganza. He also developed his cast of characters. Offisa Bull Pupp (who in earlier strips could be a mailman or a baker rather than a cop), Mrs. Kwakk-Wak, Joe Stork, the Krazy Katbird, and the Krazy Katfish, Ignatz's wife and kids, and many others all contributed their share of krazy kapers to both the daily and Sunday strips.

Krazy Kat is, on one level, a cat and mouse story, although in this version the mouse harasses the cat and not, as is common, vice versa. And too, it is a dog-and-cat story, although, again the story is twisted, and the dog protects, rather than chases, the cat.

But, more than anything, *Krazy Kat* is about love. Krazy loves, period. She (or he or it—in Krazy's world, the realities of gender are of little importance) loves Ignatz because it is in her nature to love. Ignatz loves her, although he wouldn't admit it, because, since he is part of Krazy's world, it is also in his nature to love. And Offisa Pup loves Krazy because what else is there but love? Once you leave the trivialities of our world behind, you enter Krazy's world of emotion, where love and joy reign. This is the world Herriman brings to us, portrayed against a surreal American desert.

Opposite: Krazy Kat was such a favorite that she starred in a jazz-pantomine ballet by John Alden Carpenter, for which Herriman created the scenario, scenery, and costumes. It was first performed at the Town Hall, New York City, in 1922. Here Krazy performs a pas de chat in this illustration from the rare, original score.

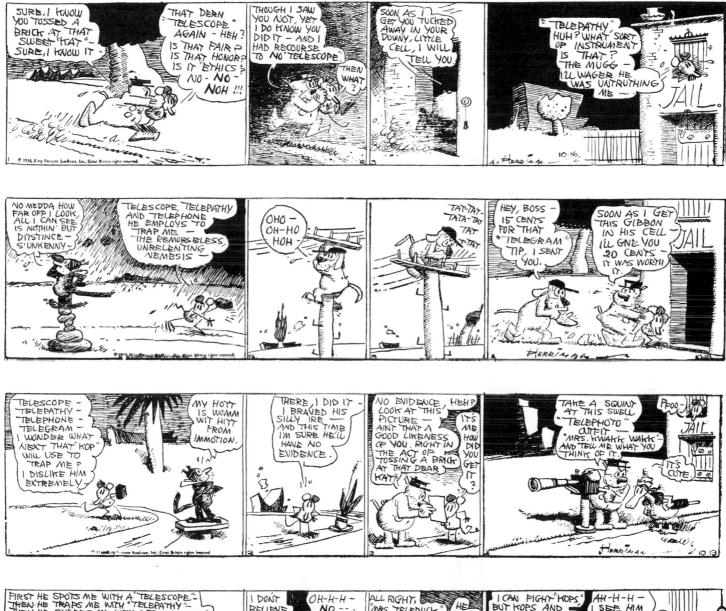

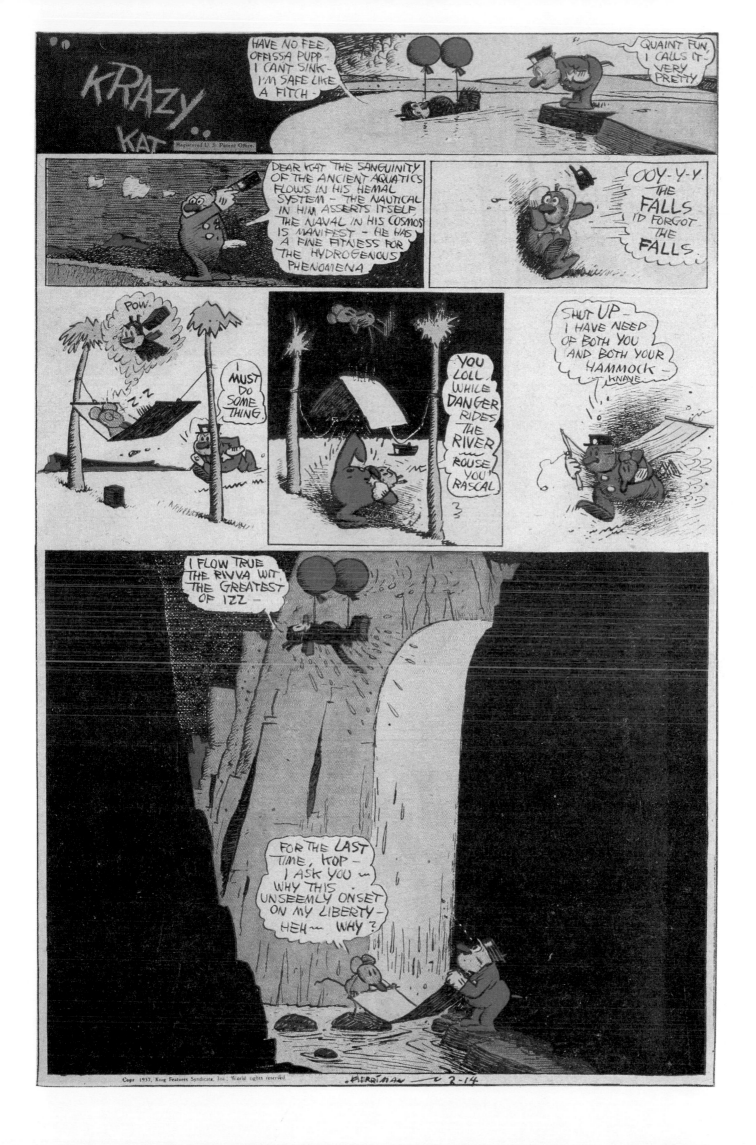

FELIX

Felix the Cat, the first comic strip character to be seen initially on the screen, then in the comics, is credited to Pat Sullivan, who operated the animation studio releasing the Felix cartoons in the 1920s. Actually, Felix was probably the invention of Otto Messmer, a Sullivan employee who drew both the animated Felix and the strip Felix until 1954 when Joe Oriolo took over.

Messmer aimed the strip primarily at youngsters, with simple, gag-studded continuity, but it appealed as well to those adults who had an eye for a fine comic line and detail. The strip continued to use the bold, easy-to-see style of art that characterized the movies. *Felix the Cat* was a widely admired strip, and fans followed the cat from the comic page into the original Felix comic books, onto the TV screen, and then to the stores for the numerous toys, games, and dolls the strip gave birth to.

Despite all the trials and tribulations he would face from one strip to the next, Felix still managed to laugh at himself and the world around him. He spent his most exciting adventures in lands of myth and daydreams, where comic fantasy and comic strip reality often crossed paths. To escape from the clutches of his enemies or to win the love of his Phyllis, Felix used any tool available, often including parts of the strip itself. Speech balloons could be emptied and used as parachutes; exclamation points could be used to conk enemies over the head. Felix even found that his tail was removable and could be used as comic prop or weapon, depending on what the situation called for.

But, despite the fantastical aspects of the strip, Felix was one of the most catlike comic cats. Like Kipling's "The Cat That Walked by Himself," he is practical and self-sufficient, yet he longs for human companions and a home. And it was that true desire that brought people and cats together in the first place.

POLLY AND HER PALS

Never a cat strip *per se*, Cliff Sterrett's greatly admired *Polly and Her Pals* strip was the next best thing—a strip in which a cat was a vital part of the action, a major and pivotal character from one year to the next. In this case, Kitty was the constant companion of Paw Perkins, the strip's central figure (despite its title), and she was developed graphically in the bizarre, individual manner that characterized all of Sterrett's drawing. Paw, the father of the titular Polly, and Kitty were usually involved in some domestic problem set in motion by the conflict, implicit or actual, always extant between Paw and Maw Perkins.

Kitty Perkins mirrored Paw's every move and emotion, supporting his shows of strength, aping his exasperation at the emancipated Polly, and scurrying away the minute anyone challenged Paw's illusory head-of-the household powers. The fact that these attitudes wore as well on Kitty as on Paw just enhanced the comical aspects of the strip.

Of course, the art itself was a major part of the strip. During its peak, Sterrett's art was the epitome of cartoon Art Deco, echoing the period's style in all the panel's furnishings and fashions. He carried on the artistic tradition started in *Krazy Kat*, incorporating elements of cubism and surrealism into very human situations. Kitty himself was a perfect combination of wild stylization and exact, angular lines. It is no wonder that *Polly and Her Pals* lasted almost 50 years.

CICERO'S CAT

Cicero's Cat, like *Krazy Kat*, started out as a tailpiece for a larger comic feature. Although bylined by Bud Fisher, it was invented by Al Smith, a ghost on Fisher's *Mutt and Jeff* strip. Cicero, of the strip's title, was Mutt's son; the cat, who shortly took over the entire Sunday feature, was named Desdemona.

Desi, as she was known, is one of the most human of comic strip cats. Her face is as human as any of the characters; the cat body seems to be just a costume that'll come off any moment. Also, Desi often wore clothes to further enhance the duality of her appearance. But Desi is all cat. She is sly, tricky, vulnerable, and very funny. Combining the amusing antics that characterize all comic cats with slapstick style, Desi is one of the most continually amusing of all the *Mutt and Jeff* characters.

At first, Fisher's initial strip, *A. Mutt* (1907-1909), met with resistance from some readers. His style was too coarse, too cruel, too real perhaps. The art, certainly on a different level than *Krazy Kat* or *Polly and Her Pals*, was said to be simply badly drawn doodles. People resented Fisher's shortcuts: dotted lines from a man's eyes to the object he was viewing; a few straight lines to indicate action, some stars to accompany a knock on the head.

But Fisher knew what he was doing. He didn't care to keep everyone amused every day, as long as *someone* was amused. He knew that, even if you weren't interested in one strip, you'd keep reading anyway, just to figure out why your neighbor was yelping with laughter. And his plan worked. The strip continued to grow, was plagiarized until legal action stopped that, and carried on by Al Smith even after Fisher died. Everyone knows Mutt and Jeff, and Desdemona has certainly earned her place in the comic cat hall of fame.

CICERO'S CAT

If You Can't Make Up Your Mind Someone Else Will!

THE PUSSYCAT PRINCESS

Easily the most densely populated cat strip of all was Grace G. Drayton's *The Pussycat Princess*, whose title character presided affectionately over an entire kingdom of cats. Drayton, who was most famous for the Campbell Kids she created for the Campbell Soup Company, was also known for her Dolly Dingle paper dolls, children's book illustrations, fashion pages, magazine covers, and the toys, dolls and stuffed animals that she designed. In the late 1920s, she drew, for the Hearst papers, a strip called *Dolly Dimples and Bobby Bounce*. This continued as both a daily and a Sunday page feature until the more attractive *Pussycat Princess* concept occurred to Drayton. That strip was launched as a new, Sunday only, feature in 1934.

The strip was written by Edward Anthony and later drawn by Ruth Carroll, but Drayton's style was the strip's trademark. All of her creations, people and cats, were characterized by round bodies, chubby cheeks, and the famous curved-H mouth. Some comic-watchers have suggested that they were modeled after Drayton herself.

Anthony knew what people love most about language, and he built his text around the jokes, puns, riddles, and rhymes that keep readers laughing. The strips usually had some type of punchline, with perhaps just a bit of a moral. Good always won, and, in fact, a reader would learn, there is good in every cat.

Although the cats did everything that people do and more, the population of the pussycat kingdom retained at least a vestige of their catness, preferring fish above all other delicacies and meowing constantly. Incredibly cuddly and obviously fun, they drew millions of children and adults into a land of fantasy and myth. The last strip appeared in July 1947.

SPOOKY

Bill Holman's madly inspired *Spooky*, started in 1934, was originally the firehouse cat under the tangled feet of Smokey Stover and Chief Cash U. Nutt in the earliest *Smokey Stover* Sunday page episodes. Once the *Smokey Stover* feature began national distribution, however, a second strip was added to the Sunday layout, and Smokey's obstreperous cat became its leading character. Spooky is almost wholly anarchistic in behavior, utterly self-centered, and sublimely violent in action—in short, she is the complete cat of everyone's experience, elevated to a surreal presentation. Known for her red-bandaged tail, she skipped blithely through a madcap setting, leaving destruction and bemusement in her wake.

Comical doesn't even *begin* to describe the strip as a whole, however. Holman made use of sight gags, puns, nonsense words and phrases (his most famous being "Foo," "notary sojac," and "1506 nix nix"), exaggeration and fantasy. Like Gene Ahern and George Swan before him, he broke all the rules for drawing comic strips. The panels looked more like pieces of a jigsaw puzzle than squares, and they often couldn't entirely contain their subjects, so that tails, hands and various other props often intruded into other spaces. Various framed pictures, usually captioned by groan-invoking puns, appeared throughout the strip, simply as decoration or as a comic panel within a comic strip.

Spooky ran as an independent strip until 1945, when it was reincorporated into *Smokey Stover*. By the mid-1950s, it was out of print.

THE CAT & THE KID

A comic needn't be famous to be great, as *The Cat and the Kid* proves. Often a fine example of a pantomine feature, its gentle humor and homey setting can make even the most modern reader nostalgic.

Very little is known about the author or the strip itself. It started in the *Philadelphia Evening Ledger* around 1935 and lasted about two years. John Rosol, the artist, dropped out of sight.

Pantomine cartoons were the comic world's answer to Charlie Chaplin and his movies. Featuring characters who rarely, if ever, spoke, they were loved by children and adults because they were easy to understand and even nonreaders could enjoy them.

One of the first pantomine feature strips was *Benny*, which was started in 1931 by J. Carver Pusey and featured a Chaplinesque character. It was followed in 1932 by *Henry*, which is about a silent, bald-headed, artful young man.

The Cat and the Kid featured a cat who looked like a stuffed animal come alive and a little boy who resembled the baby brother everybody wanted but rarely got. Both were cute, snuggly, well-behaved and quiet. Mother and father were storybook parents—calm, kind, and loving. The house was plain but neat, furnished with everything a middle-class family might want. In short, here was a household everyone could admire and long for, expecially during the impoverished depression years.

The cat, while not particularly anthropomorphic, still managed to hold her own in a world of people. The strip's humor centered around the loving relationship between the cat and the boy. They never did anything too out of the ordinary; in fact, part of the intended appeal of the strip was its mirroring of everyday life. It's a shame that the strip was never able to reach the audience it was intended for.

THE CAT AND THE KID

Registered U. S. Patent Office

Chapter 7   CAT TALES

Book Illustration from 1915 to the Present

It's a long way from the schoolroom hornbook of the late 18th century to the full-color illustrated children's books of today, but the thrust of the two forms has never wavered: to prepare young people for the world they will come to know. To this purpose, throughout the past two hundred years, the cat image has been a constant, familiar, friendly guide.

Even through two world wars, experimentation and progress in publishing childen's books has continued. Printing processes have become so sophisticated that reproduction of almost any type of artwork is possible. In 1921, *The Newbery Award* for best story and, in 1938, *The Caldecott Medal* for best illustrations were established for children's books. These awards recognize the importance of children's books, and competition for the prizes has spurred a wondrous outpouring of excellent art and writing.

After World War II, a tide of paperback books swept across the world, making classic children's books inexpensive and more popular. Other forms of communication flourished during this time so that a children's favorite, such as A.A. Milne's *Winnie the Pooh* as retold by Walt Disney, could be first read in a paperback book, comic book, or newspaper strip and then seen as a movie or television program. Tigger, Christopher Robin's feline chum, bounded happily through all these forms.

Opposite: From British cartoonist Ronald Searle's book, Searles's Cats, *this pussycat portrait is captioned: "Young cat already regretting puberty."*

Right: Singing cat and long-suffering mouse by Garth Williams.

Above: New Yorker *cartoonist Richard Decker illus-trated H.H. (Saki) Munro's classic cat ghost story* "Tobermory" *for* The Golden Book Magazine, *1931.*

Opposite, above: This endless undulation of cats originally appeared in Wanda Gag's famed children's book, Millions of Cats, *which won a Newbery Award in 1934. Opposite, below: A 1928 children's opus called* The Raggedy Animal Book, *boasts drawings by Harrison Cady, an early contributor to St. Nicholas.*

The Raggedy Cat singing her evening song

THE CAT AND THE MOUSE

HE cat and the mouse

Play'd in the malt-house:

 The cat bit the mouse's tail off. "Pray, puss, give me my tail."

 "No," says the cat, "I'll not give you your tail till you go to the cow and fetch me some milk."

  First she leapt, and then she ran,

  Till she came to the cow, and thus began:

 "Pray, Cow, give me milk, that I may give cat milk, that cat may give me my tail again."

Above: American book and magazine illustrator, Frederick Richardson, had so individual a style that the many issues of Child Life *he illustrated in the 1930s were marked as uniquely his own. Here he draws a pleasing layout for a page in* Frederick Richardson's Book For Children, *1938. Below: Leonard Leslie Brooke did not often draw cats, but, when this fabled British children's book illustrator did undertake the subject (as here, in rendering the Crooked Man's crooked cat in* Ring O'Roses, A Nursery Rhyme Picture Book), *he was inimitable.*

Tigers, toy and real. Above: Frederick Richardson's rendition from his Book For Children, 1938. Below: World-acclaimed English illustrator and cartoonist Ernest Howard Shepard, who worked much of the time for Punch, is noted primarily for his matchless illustrations in A.A. Milne's Winnie the Pooh books. The series' only cat character, a stuffed tiger toy named Tigger, shared his adventures with all the other toy characters.

117

are you abducting me, Percy?

Everyone who gave the matter any serious thought at all realized from the beginning that Don Marquis's inimitable *archy and mehitabel*, could only be illustrated by the unexcelled cat artist of the time, George Herriman. By the time Marquis's second collection of verses about his cockroach (*archy*) and cat (*mehitabel*) had been published, arrangements had been made, and both the first two books, as well as a culminating third, carried a bounteous array of Herriman drawings. The three were soon incorporated into a single anthology, which has never gone out of print since its acclaimed appearance in the early 1930s. It is a classic for children and adults.

118

Another kind of cross-over occurred when one of the great comic artist's work would jump from the funny papers to the book world. *Krazy Kat* illustrator, George Herriman, for instance, brought to life the fabled archie and his cat crony, mehitabel. Herriman's insight into the characters and his rendering of them fixed their likenesses forever in the reader's mind. Milt Gross, irrepressible father of such nutty strips as *Count Screwloose of Tooloose, Nize Baby,* and *That's My Pop!* illustrated an equally riotous book, *Pasha the Persian,* featuring the comic adventures of a pedigreed Persian cat on the rough-and-tumble sidewalks of New York.

No matter where their art finally appears, the artists and writers of 20th century children's literature continue, with only ink on paper, to magically create characters that live. Whether folk stories, educational and moral lessons, or just plain entertainment, the principals of these cat tales for children continue to be highly original, endlessly amusing, and solidly companionable—just like the real thing.

"WELL, FLATTEN MY EARS—IF IT AIN'T DE PRINCE OF PARK AVENOO!!"

Possibly the most rascally, knowingly sophisticated, and rough and tumble of all drawn cats are those created by the American cartoonist, Milt Gross, for the now unfortunately rare 1936 Pasha the Persian, by Margaret Linden. These two illustrations catch the frantic comic range of this lovely work. Gross, as well liked for his ethnic comic prose as for his cartoons, wrote several other best-sellers, including Hiawatta Witt No Odder Poems, 1926, De Night In De Front From Chreesmas, 1927, *and* Famous Fimmales Witt Odder Ewents From Heestory, 1928.

Children's books during the 1950s benefited from the ever increasing improvements in printing techniques. These adorable kittens were painted by Feodor Rojonkovsky for The Giant Golden Book of Cat Stories, 1953 by Elizabeth Coatsworth.

Left: Garth Williams's loving treatment of cats is evident in this composition from the children's classic, The Cricket in Times Square, 1960. Below: Williams tackles a mouse tackling a cat in these illustrations from Harry Cat's Pet Puppy, 1974. Both books were written by George Selden.

Obviously, this grimly glowering kitten of Caldecott Award-winning artist Tomi Ungerer's is refusing mother so much as a pleasant look, and the prospect of a kiss is nil. These illustrations are from No Kiss For Mother, 1973, which you will have to read to learn if Mother ever gets a kiss.

Piper does not wash because he does not like to.
He does not like to brush his teeth either.
When he reaches the bathroom,
he promptly latches the door to keep his mother out.
He turns on the water, lets it run, and wets his washcloth.
Then he rubs his toothbrush on the edge of the sink.
"In case Mother Snoop is listening," Piper says.
Then he takes it easy for a while,
looking at some soggy comic books
which he keeps behind the tub.

Left: This delightfully decorative pet graces The Fat Cat Coloring and Limerick Book. *Donna Sloan created the imaginative drawings, while Malcolm Whyte furnished the accompanying limericks, such as the following for the Fat Cat:*

A fat cat in his elegant house
When asked what fancy foods he'd espouse
Replied: "I'm quite keen
On Trout Amandine
And I've lost my taste for the mouse.

Below: Certainly as fat a cat as ever waddled through a children's book, this enormously satisfied feline is from Jack Kent's retelling of a Danish folktale, The Fat Cat, *1971. Kent, who created the greatly enjoyed* King Aroo *comic strip of some years ago, has recently focused his talent on children's books. (The cat is fat, incidentally, because he has been gobbling up everyone in sight; however, all survive happily at the end, including the fat cat himself.)*

Next he met five birds in a flock.
And they said to him, "What have you
been eating, my little cat? You are so fat."

If there is one artist who obviously loves cats, to own or to draw, it's Edward Gorey. Having authored and illustrated over sixty books, including fairy tales, ABCs and deliciously macabre mystery stories, Gorey reputedly lives with several cats in his New England retreat. The cats on these pages were done as a diptych for The Cat Catalog, 1976.

Cheerleading cat with crepe paper chrysanthemums

Cats taking a barre ▮ in all sorts of lumpy ▮ and subfusc garments — traditional for this endeavour

124

who appeared in the | left half of the diptych | on the opposite page | Thought up by Edw. Gorey

as the first seventeen cats | Cat practicing sleeve gestures | of Life to the world in general | readings of a dismal nature | in the air above a croquet wicket

Commedia dell' arte | Cat semaphoring *A Psalm* | Cat giving tarot card | Spectral cat appearing

are as bafflingly occupied | cance in honour of the rising sun | a fashionable skating rink

A group of cats who | have gotten up in the | dark to do a garland | Cat being nonchalant at

in which seventeen other cats | be extinguished in a pantry | a hitherto unknown overture | the finale but also curtain calls

Famous cat burglar | waiting for a light to | Cat about to conduct

Right half of the same diptych | raisin cookies on the back porch | caught by a sudden gust of wind | of a rustico-ethnic persuasion | wires will hold during not only

Cat juggling impromptu | Another butterfly cat | Cat in a comic recitation | Cat wondering if the

Edward Gorey

125

Chapter 8 CONTEMPORARY CATS
Comic Strip Cats from 1939 to the Present

Why are cats eternally popular? Perhaps because they are a lot more like humans than we'd care to admit. Their comportment is one of aloofness, supple grace, and absolute self-control. Cats are pillars of aplomb. They are also comical. They'll jump a mile when startled, then try to look cool. Langorous poise unravels into fretfulness at a not-too-distant bark. Cats sleep, stretch, yawn, and scratch funny. They clown endlessly with any kind of bric-a-brac, but still take their play seriously. We recognize the duality of their nature and smile at the reflection. With *comic* cats the balance is tipped just a smidgen to the silly side, making them instantly funny and endearing—a happy encounter in an ever perplexing world.

Comic cats, like all of us, grew up after World War II. The simple cat-and-mouse comedy of Mickey Mouse and the cuddly cuteness of Walt Disney's Figaro (in the animated film of *Pinocchio*) gave way to either subtle sophistication or raw feline fiendishness.

Although a direct reference to Nast's merciless tiger, Walt Kelly's Mr. Tammanany (from the brilliant *Pogo* strip) is really a soul of generous mien and thus an engaging satire on his namesake. George Booth's cats in the *New Yorker* are some of the most domestic, but urbanely comic, ever published. Gordo's cat, Poosy Gato, is another instance of both sophisticated humor and design—as is the whole strip.

Movie cats, such as Tom of *Tom and Jerry*, Sylvester, and even some of the later Disney cats, joined their print pals Heathcliff and Garfield in offering plenty of slapstick humor, but with a devilish edge to it.

Opposite: Comic cats from 1939 to present: Above: Figaro from Walt Disney's 1939 movie Pinocchio. *Below: Garfield from today's comic strips.*

Right: Pat from Nard n' Pat *by Jay Lynch.*

BUGS BUNNY

Film cartoon cats: Above: Bugs Bunny's fast talking buddy. Sylvester the cat.
Below: Jerry lights one up for Tom. Opposite: Walt Disney's cat collection:
Above, left: Lucifer in an animated sequence from Cinderella. Above, right:
Two Siamese, if you please, from Lady and The Tramp. Below: The classic
cat and mouse of the cartoons, Mickey and his feline nemesis, Peg Leg Pete.

POGO

Newspaper strip cats: Opposite: Mr. Tammanany enlivens a series from the always lively Pogo *by Walt Kelly. Above: Motley muses mutely in the contemporary strip,* Wright Angles *by Larry Wright. Below: Never a dull moment in* Heathcliff *by George Gately.*

For really grown-up comic cats, we must explore the "underground" comics. Here is earthy fun, social comment, flinty pathos, and experimental art all in one. Fritz the Cat lives a ribald life of dissipation and conscious-stricken abandon. Fat Freddie's cat is gross, hip, and a comic riot. Pat, from *Nard 'n Pat*, is a lusty, convivial cat, reminiscent of Mr. Jack, only Pat gets the girl occasionally.

Thus, from the first comic cat to the newest we see them mirroring our lives. They act out our folly, our needs, and our frustrations with style and steadfast amiability. And with the ingenious artists who create them, the merry graphic tabbies daily give us joy. It is good to know that as long as there are people to draw them and an audience to appreciate them, we will always be surrounded by those curious, querulous, quixotic comic cats.

"AH, GOOD!...NO SIGN OF HEATHCLIFF!"

"I STEPPED ON HIS TAIL."

© 1968, Jay Lynch

Magazine cats: Above: From the underground comix (official underground spelling) comes Pat the cat, from Nard n' Pat, skillfully drawn by Jayzey Lynch.

Opposite: George Booth's droll cartoons from the New Yorker often teem with funny furry fixtures.

"Edgar, please run down to the shopping center right away, and get some milk and cat food. Don't get canned tuna, or chicken, or liver or any of those awful combinations. Shop around and get a surprise. The pussies like surprises."

GORDO

Gustavo (Gus) Arriola's bed-lounging, table-clawing, window-vaulting Poosy Gato (comic strip Mexican for "pussycat") shares the center stage spotlight in the daily and Sunday strip *Gordo*® with a rooster, a dog, a pig, and an owl, to say nothing of Gordo and his human cronies, some inebriated worms, and a spider. Arriola deftly plays with basic cat instincts to move everyday situations out of the ordinary and into the amusing. A cat scratching a piece of furniture is not funny; Poosy Gato being pulled by his very nature to scratch the *most expensive* piece of furniture, is.

The secret lives of pets are also brought to the fore in *Gordo*®. When Poosy is with Gordo or other humans, he is pure cat—meowing, scratching, sleeping, chasing birds, climbing onto the softest lap available. However, when he is with other animals, he talks, jokes, teases and philosophizes, and so do they.

Gordo® first appeared in 1941 but was suspended when Arriola was drafted into the wartime army. Obviously drawn to comic illustrating the way Poosy is drawn to catnip, Arriola soon arranged to do his Sunday strip despite his military obligations. His daily strip returned in 1946, when he was discharged.

At first, the strip was mainly about Gordo, a small-time farmer (he now owns a tour bus), the Widow Gonzales, who did her best to lead Gordo down the aisle, and various other humans. More recently, the Sunday strip has been almost entirely given over to the animal population. Arriola has added two more cats to his lineup: an adult black cat named P.M. and Bete Noire, a tiny black kitten who keeps the adult cats as amused as the strip's readers. These strips depend on eye-pleasing design and simple gags, rather than the narrative that characterized the earlier daily strips. Delightful in and of themselves, the strips also hold a little extra surprise each week for those who know where to look (for those who don't, check the byline under the title in the Sunday strips).

GORDO   **By Gus Arriola**

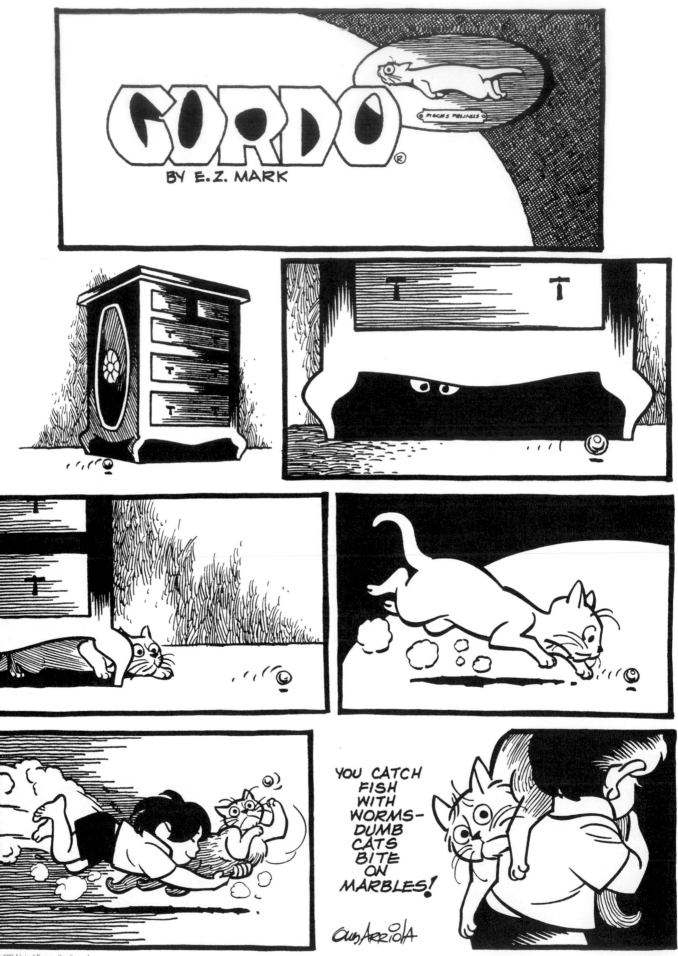

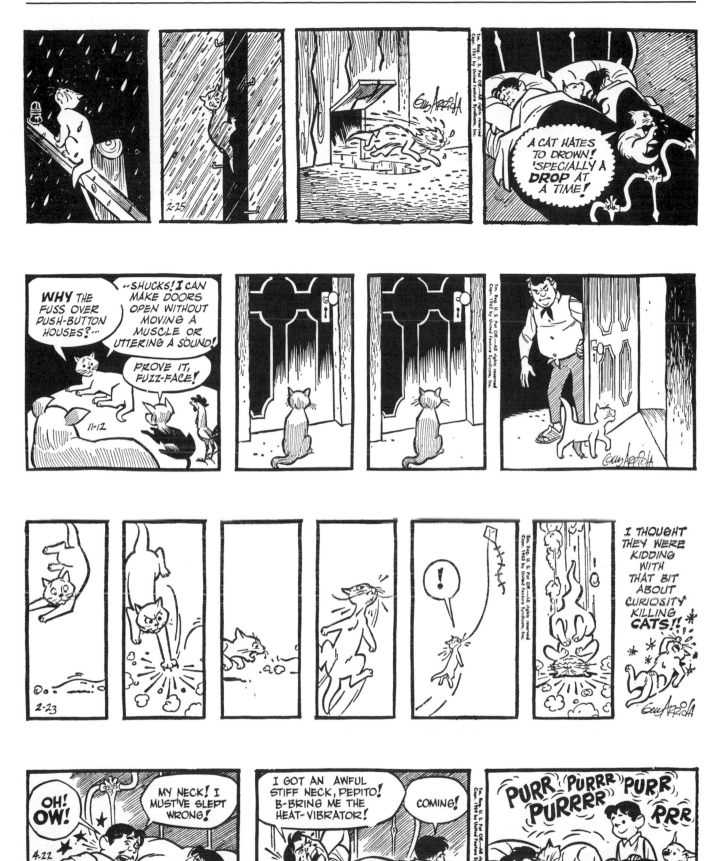

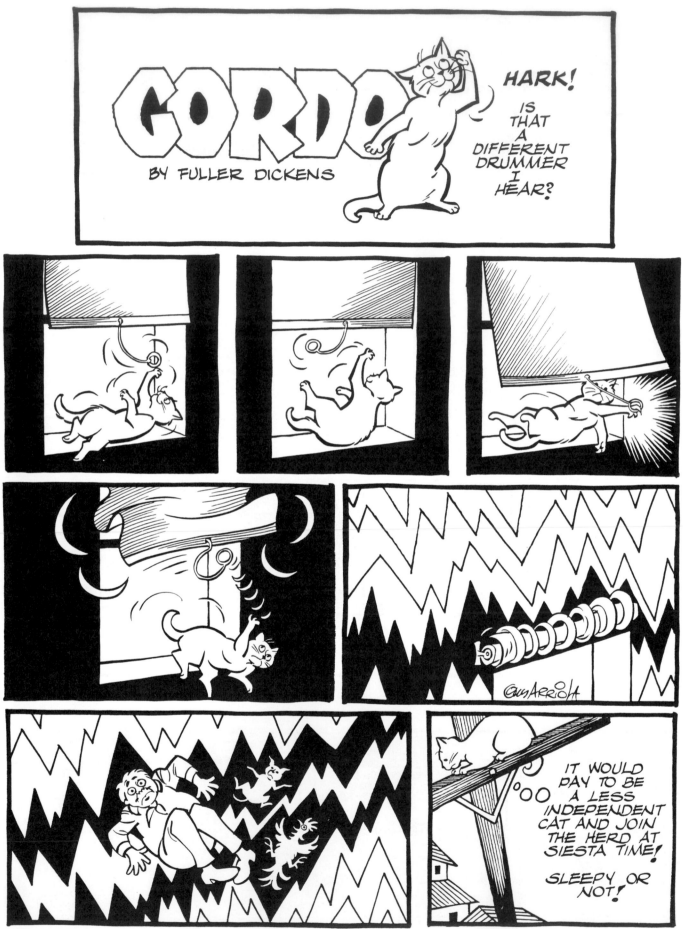

FRITZ THE CAT

In 1972, Fritz the Cat, perhaps the best-known underground "comix" character, was brutally murdered by an ostrich named Andrea. It must be admitted, however, that Fritz probably deserved his shocking end; he had gone "establishment" and had become a playboy movie star, hanging around with big-shot Hollywood producers. And, the ostrich contended, he had forced her to degrade herself for him and perform acts that would make even the most lustful bird blush.

Fritz was created in 1959 by Robert Crumb for a private comic book produced by Crumb and his brother Charles. Originally, the cat was based on Crumb's pet cat Fred, but Charles's comic characters started calling him Fritz, and the name stuck. In 1964, a Fritz strip appeared in *Help!*, a humor magazine edited by *Mad* magazine's Harvey Kurtzman. Fritz strips were collected and published in book form in 1968 and 1969, although by then Crumb had gone on to other ventures.

Fritz was not your average feline. He was a feisty, vulgar, irresponsible, insecure, drug-crazed sex fiend, often involved in illegal and riotous activities. With humor and understanding, Crumb used Fritz to not-so-gently satirize the soul-searching 60's with its promises of total freedom accompanied by heavy doses of guilt.

But, like many other 60's heroes, Fritz was appropriated by businessmen who recognized a salable item when they saw one. In 1969, producers Ralph Bakshi and Steve Krantz discussed with Crumb the possibility of making an animated movie of Fritz. Although Crumb says he never agreed to the project, the film was made and released in 1972 without Crumb's name on it. Aware that Fritz was being misused, Crumb executed Fritz with a stroke of his pen and disassociated himself from all other Fritz projects. Fritz's untimely demise was certainly unique in the history of comic cats, but then, so was Fritz.

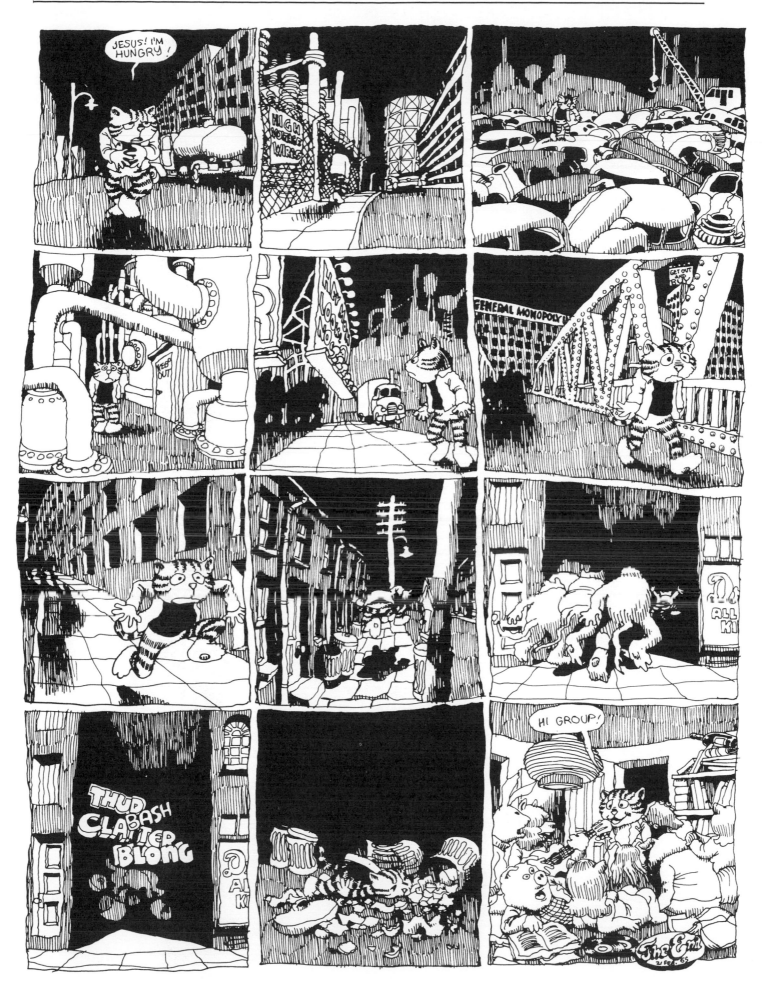

FAT FREDDY'S CAT

Fat Freddy's Cat first appeared as a tailpiece to Gilbert Shelton's *The Fabulous Furry Freak Brothers.* That strip, starring Fat Freddy, Freewheelin' Franklin, and Phineas Freak, has, along with Crumb's *Fritz the Cat* and *Mr. Natural,* transcended the world of underground comix to find its place in the realms of mainstream comics. It is funny, entertaining, and germane. The strip first appeared in the *Los Angeles Free Press,* then moved to comic books where it reached a circulation of over 100,000.

Fat Freddy's Cat is all tomcat. Shelton, with great comic effect, created a cat who is vivacious and exciting, with moves that would put an acrobat to shame. The epitome of realism, he is scruffy, scrawny, and explicitly detailed. He relieves himself in the most awkward places, messes up the entire house in search of food, and eats the marijuana plants the brothers so lovingly cultivate. But, like any cat owner, Fat Freddy can never get too angry at his cat who is also silly, sensitive and affectionate.

Fat Freddie's Cat, unlike Cicero's, is somewhat more a creature of the alley than the hearth—it would be difficult, in fact, to find anything around Fat Freddy's pad that could be said to approximate a hearth. Even at home, Fat Freddie's Cat (who seems to have no other name) has an uphill struggle to face every day: Fat Freddy rarely puts out food unless the alert cat claws his leg, the food itself may vary from mashed potatoes to toast crusts, and even this has to be defended against mice and cockroaches. But, in spite of household conditions of such Oliver Twist dimensions, Fat Freddie's Cat remains loyal—although he is markedly deficient in many of the other Scout manual traits, such as being trustworthy, obedient, and reverent. These Fat Freddie's Cat decidedly is not. He is, however, everybody's favorite tomcat translated into a recognizable, although somewhat freakish, comic character.

GARFIELD

Garfield® by Jim Davis is the newest addition to the legions of cartoon pussycats. First syndicated in 1978, the strip quickly became one of the most widely read newspaper features, earning two best-selling books of its own.

Garfield is so popular because he's everything we would be if only we could let ourselves go. He is fat, lazy, grumpy, and cynical. He eats almost constantly, and, when he isn't eating, he's sleeping. There are no sacred cows for Garfield; he looks out for himself at all times. These traits, however, are not really why he is loved so much. Beneath his somewhat cool exterior, he is childlike, easily frightened, and loving. He expresses our thoughts, emotions, and desires. Of course, he is also very funny.

Sharing the strip with Garfield are Jon Arbuckle, his owner (based on Davis himself), and Jon's flaky roommate, Lyman. The fourth member of the household is Lyman's dog Odie, who plays the role of Garfield's ofttimes enemy, sometimes partner-in-crime. Odie is all dog, running around with his tongue hanging out and a blissful but vacant expression. Rounding out the cast of characters are various girlfriends, a lady vet, and a mailman, all of whom are fair game for Garfield.

The strip is visually simple, drawn with bold, sure lines and little clutter. The daily strips always follow the same format of three equal-sized squares; the outside two boxed in and the middle one left open. The gags are straightforward and easy to understand, so that every cat and comic lover can share in Garfield's silliness.

Because he is so catlike and yet so human, because the strip is so easily accessible to all readers, Garfield's reign promises to be a long one as he takes his place alongside Krazy, Felix, Kitty Perkins, Desi, Spooky, Poosy Gato and all the other great comic cats.

BIBLIOGRAPHY

Becker, Stephen, *Comic Art in America.* New York: Simon and Schuster, 1959.

Blackbeard, Bill and Williams, Martin, eds., *The Smithsonian Collection of Newspaper Comics.* New York: Smithsonian Institute Press/Harry N. Abrams, 1977.

Craven, Thomas, ed., *Cartoon Cavalcade.* New York: Simon and Schuster, 1933.

Feaver, William, *When We Were Young.* New York: Holt, Rinehart and Winston, 1977.

Fireman, Judy, *The Cat Catalog.* New York: Workman Publishing Co., 1976.

George, M. Dorothy, *Hogarth to Cruikshank: Social Change in Graphic Satire.* New York: Walker and Co., 1967.

Havilan, Virginia and Coughlan, Margaret N., *Yankee Doodle's Literary Sampler of Prose, Poetry and Pictures, selected from the Rare Book Collection of the Library of Congress.* New York: Thomas Y. Crowell Co., 1974.

Horn, Maurice, ed., *The World Encyclopedia of Comics.* New York: Chelsea House Publishers, 1976.

James, Philip, *Children's Books of Yesterday.* London: The Studio Ltd., 1933.

Kunzle, David, *The Early Comic Strips.* Berkeley: University of California Press, 1973.

Paine, Albert Bigelow, *Th. Nast: His Period and His Pictures.* New York: Harper and Brothers, 1904.

Perry, George and Aldridge, Alan, *The Penguin Book of Comics.* Middlesex: Penguin Books Ltd., 1967.

Robinson, Jerry, *The Comics.* New York: Berkley Publishing Corp., 1974.

Suares, Jean-Claude and Chwast, Seymour, *The Illustrated Cat.* New York: PushPin Press/Harmony Books, 1976.

Tuer, Andrew W., *Forgotten Children's Books.* London: The Leadenhill Press, Ltd., 1898.

Waugh, Coulton, *The Comics.* New York: MacMillan, 1974.

From The Household Stories by the Brothers Grimm, *pictures by Walter Crane, translated by Lucy Crane, MacMillan & Co., 1886.*

INDEX

"The Cat That Walked By Himself," from
Just So Stories *by Rudyard Kipling.*